MODERN HUMANITIES RESEARCH ASSOCIATION

CRITICAL TEXTS

VOLUME 20

Editor
MALCOLM COOK
(*French*)

LE PARADIS PERDU

by

Évariste-Désiré de Parny

LE PARADIS PERDU

by

Évariste-Désiré de Parny

Edited by
Ritchie Robertson and Catriona Seth

MODERN HUMANITIES RESEARCH ASSOCIATION
2009

Published by

The Modern Humanities Research Association,
1 Carlton House Terrace
London SW1Y 5AF

© The Modern Humanities Research Association, 2009

Ritchie Robertson and Catriona Seth have asserted their right under the Copyright, Designs and Patents Act 1988 to be identified as the authors of this work.

Parts of this work may be reproduced as permitted under legal provisions for fair dealing (or fair use) for the purposes of research, private study, criticism, or review, or when a relevant collective licensing agreement is in place. All other reproduction requires the written permission of the copyright holder who may be contacted at rights@mhra.org.uk.

First published 2009

ISBN 978 0 947623 90 6

ISSN 1746-1642

Copies may be ordered from www.criticaltexts.mhra.org.uk

Table of Contents

Introduction 1

Le Paradis perdu 49

Further Reading 89

Introduction

Évariste Désiré de Parny (1753–1814)

Few people nowadays are familiar with the name of Parny. Even in his native Réunion, where the odd school or road is called after him, one would be hard pressed to find someone able to quote from his works. The best bet would certainly be to ask a musician: Ravel's justly famous *Chansons madécasses* are settings of three prose poems which the French author published in 1787. So, who was Parny? He who, in his day, was both fêted and reviled; famous for love poems which enchanted readers such as the young Chateaubriand, Pushkin and Lamartine; but also renowned for anticlerical works which divided opinion?

Born on 6 February 1753 and baptized the next day by Father Monet in the parish church of Saint-Paul in the Île Bourbon (as Réunion was then known), Évariste-Désiré was the second son of Paul Parny and his second wife, née Geneviève de Lanux. His mother died before his fourth birthday.[1] Described as 'écuyer, lieutenant d'infanterie', his father had served in the French army in India and owned some land and a few slaves. The family was by no means one of the richest on the island. At Geneviève Parny's death they owned some thirty books, essentially practical treatises on mathematics or fortifications and devotional texts.

We know nothing specific about the writer's early education. Schooling on the Île Bourbon was left either to the Lazarists or to slaves and the occasional drunken soldier, if we are to believe Parny himself:

> On ne se doute pas dans notre île de ce que c'est que l'éducation. L'enfance est l'âge qui demande de la part des parents le plus de prudence et le plus de soin ; ici l'on abandonne les enfants aux mains des esclaves ; ils prennent insensiblement les goûts et les mœurs de ceux avec qui ils vivent ; aussi à la couleur près, le maître ressemble parfaitement à l'esclave. À sept ans, quelque soldat ivrogne leur apprend à lire, à écrire, et leur enseigne les quatre premières règles de l'arithmétique, alors l'éducation est complète.

Parny spent his first ten years on Bourbon. In August 1763, like the sons of most of the Creoles, as the white settlers were known, he was packed off to France to further his education. He was entrusted, along with his two brothers, Jean-Baptiste, the elder, and Chériseuil, the younger, to a Breton woman, Rose Pinczon du Sel. She was travelling back to Brittany with her own children, Auguste, a contemporary of Évariste, who was to remain a firm friend until his untimely death, and Marie-Anne. They were on board the *Condé*, a 50-cannon warship which had been part of the comte d'Aché's squadron sent to India, for over four months before docking in Lorient on 12 January 1764. Rose Pinczon du Sel and the five children then headed off to Rennes, her home town, where the boys were to be sent to school.

The Collège de Rennes had been one of the Jesuits' famed urban institutions, though by the time Évariste and his brothers arrived there, the Order had been expelled from France. Term had started on 16 October with a solemn mass in the presence of the town authorities. The abbé Thé du Chatellier was in charge of the 500 or so pupils. He was to show particular kindness to the young strangers who had arrived part way through the school year and from so far away. In a letter to Auguste's sister, Rosette, 'le bon du Chatellier'[2] – as Pierre-Louis Ginguené,[3] another writer who attended the Collège de Rennes, called the headmaster – remembered Jean-Baptiste's arrival at the school: 'Un marmot sort de sa coque du quartier St Paul de l'île de Bourbon en Afrique. On le dépose dans mon sein à près de 500 lieues de là. Je l'épluche et le dégrossis comme je peux.'[4]

The boys made fast progress. Évariste seems to have been good at mathematics and music. Jean-Baptiste became something of a star pupil and was awarded one of the top prizes. Du Chatellier had fond recollections of these unusual and gifted brothers:

> J'ai cultivé ces jeunes plantes de très bonne heure. Je n'y voyais constamment rien que de noble dans le cœur, l'esprit et les inclinations ; pas l'ombre des vices qui déflorent si tôt, dans les autres, l'innocence. Ils devraient être nobles, me disais-je, avec douleur, mais je vais les anoblir par une éducation complète et recherchée sans m'occuper du remboursement, ni des avances, lesquelles avec le temps me sont fidèlement rentrées ; ils furent les mieux vêtus, je leur donnai tous les maîtres, d'écriture, de danse, de musique, de violon, de mathématiques, de dessin et d'armes. Ils ont fait leurs cours d'études à pas de géant, et ont brillé et excellé en tout. Leur naturel, leur régularité ne se sont point démentis, leur réputation était affichée à Rennes, et M. de Kersalaün me dit un jour, en voyant l'aîné s'expédier avec grâce dans un exercice public, qu'il eût voulu un pareil fils, lui en dût-il coûter 60 mille [livres] pour le former. Jamais

ils n'ont abusé de ma tendresse, ni ne m'ont causé le moindre mécontentement.⁵

Parny himself recollects suffering at the hands of some of his masters and being more or less force-fed religion. On leaving Rennes, he did not, as his father seems to have wished, return to Bourbon to join the colonial forces. Instead, he went to study theology in Paris: his headmaster hoped he would become a bishop.⁶ His faith seems to have been genuine and he wrote briefly of the period in a 'Notice sur Évariste Parny' probably intended for one of his editors: 'il fut, non pas dévot, mais pieux. Ses classes faites, il vint à Paris, pour prendre l'habit ecclésiastique, et entra au séminaire de St Firmin. Pendant huit mois qu'il y resta, il étudia, il réfléchit, et sa foi s'évanouit. Il attribuait surtout *sa conversion* à la lecture de la Bible, que son confesseur lui avait toujours interdite.'⁷ The seminary's records show that he arrived on 1 September 1771 aged 18½ and left on 24 February of the following year 'pour cause de maladie'. He withdrew his belongings on 11 April. Siéyès, the future revolutionary pamphleteer, attended Saint-Firmin at the same time; he left shortly after Parny, having been ordained a deacon.⁸

Parny's brief stint as a theology student was certainly not without influence on his subsequent career as a writer. Much of his later verse is anticlerical, but shows a knowledge of the Bible which is greater than that of most of his French contemporaries. He seems to have appreciated biblical imagery and tales and, at various stages, expresses his faith in God. However, he judged the Catholic Church with considerable severity.

Exchanging his habit for a uniform, Parny joined an elite company, the Gardes du Corps de Sa Majesté, under the command of the Maréchal prince de Soubise. Taller than the minimum requirement, Parny did not fulfil another of the theoretical conditions: 'prouver quatre degrés de noblesse paternelle'. The fact that his elder half-brother and his father had served with the Gardes du Corps may have helped in waiving some of the prerequisites. Parny's life for the next few years seems to have been carefree, helped by Jean-Baptiste's great social success. The eldest of the three brothers was able to acquire an expensive but much coveted position at court, that of 'écuyer du comte d'Artois'. The Parny boys thus had direct access to the royal family. They frequented a set of talented bright young things, many of them with links to colonial France, and created a sort of dining society with mock Masonic rituals, La Caserne, which may have served as an initial hothouse for Parny's poetical talents to mature.

Everything was to change in 1773 when Paul Parny called the two younger boys back to Bourbon in order for them to seek employment as engineers or in the artillery corps. Jean-Baptiste's exalted position at Court presumably let him off the hook. He may also, at the time, have been engaged in a process which was destined to make up for the insufficient amount of blue blood which coursed through his veins. Whilst Geneviève de Lanux was of noble stock, the Parnys were not. The first one to settle on Bourbon is described in police reports as violent and ruddy, trained as a baker.[9] But, thanks to large sums of money which the family could ill afford, to his dead mother's relations[10] and to direct support from Marie-Antoinette, Jean-Baptiste was able to find 'witnesses' who swore that Pierre Parny the baker was the long-lost son of a distinguished house, the 'de Forges'. Thereafter, documents were amended and the family's name given as 'de Forges de Parny'. A number of archival elements confirm that, as Chérin, the genealogist, noted of the Parnys in the margin of his registers, 'Cette famille n'a nulle noblesse': an impoverished noble house had been only too glad to enter into an agreement with them. Added to their chronic lack of funds, this fictional genealogy meant that subsequent plans for Jean-Baptiste to marry a Breton heiress, Louise de Saint-Brice, foundered in spite of the encouragement of various well-connected friends.

Whilst all this was happening on the mainland, Évariste and Chériseuil had set out with their old friend Auguste Pinczon du Sel. They embarked on the *Laverdy* and reached Port-Louis on Mauritius some six months later, having sailed via Rio de Janeiro and spent enough time in Cape Town for Auguste to fall hopelessly in love with a Dutch Lutheran girl, Angélique Bergh. Both Parny and Auguste kept travel journals, Parny's existing in two forms, as a sort of diary and as a series of letters. Both show him experimenting with literary genres and including the odd line of verse in a prose text. The stay on the Île Bourbon, which he finally reached on 23 January 1774, was to prove the making of him as a poet.

There was an obvious aesthetic emotion on rediscovering the landscape. Parny refers, in later poems, to volcanic rocks and tropical seas. He reminds his friend Antoine de Bertin of the fruits which grow in their island home, oranges, pineapples, bananas and mangoes amongst them. Overall, though, when he refers to Bourbon, his descriptions generally show desolate surroundings which reflect his sadness. He is very critical of his compatriots and their lack of learning. He writes with feeling of the fate of the black slaves: 'Ils sont hommes, ils sont malheureux; c'est avoir bien des droits sur une âme sensible.' He deplores the fact that a man can be exchanged for a horse. Elsewhere, though, he claims slaves are treated better on Bourbon than in other colonies. He recounts an occasion on which a negro who was dying refused to be baptized by him in order not to go to a white man's afterlife where he would once again be in service. Similar anecdotes are to be found in other sources like Raynal's *Histoire des deux Indes*, and it is not clear to what extent the tale is true. Compelling evidence of Parny's split loyalties lies in the fact that not only did his family use slave labour, he personally owned at least one 'nègre', Auguste, whom he repeatedly instructed his sister to sell.[11] He also seems to have had an illegitimate daughter, Valère, with a slave-girl and to have made some provision for her dowry.[12]

Parny worked as an engineer on a project to map the island while also finding time to teach a young girl to play the harp. The music lessons, like those Danceny gives to Cécile in *Les Liaisons dangereuses*, apparently led to more intimate relations between music master and pupil. This is the stuff of Parny's first volume of verse, *Poésies érotiques*. Researchers have identified the poet's young muse, whom he calls Éléonore, as Esther Lelièvre, born on 7 June 1761, the blonde, blue-eyed daughter of a captain from the port at Saint-Paul. In spite of what seems to have been a passionate affair, to which Parny referred on numerous subsequent occasions, the young lovers did not marry. There may have been some opposition on the part of their families. Parny's father, in particular, may not have been keen for his son to get married since that would have compelled him to share out Geneviève de Lanux's inheritance with her children. Also, the Lelièvre family could boast none of the prestigious connections the Parnys had managed to acquire.

Apparently heartbroken, but in some ways delighted to be headed back for France, Parny left Bourbon on the *Seine* on 15 January 1776. Four months later, he was back with Jean-Baptiste and their friend Antoine de Bertin (1752–1790), also a poet. During Parny's absence, his brother's career had progressed considerably: he was no longer in the comte d'Artois' service. Since September 1775 he had been appointed 'écuyer de la reine' and was thus in close contact with Marie-Antoinette and her circle. He was also one of the founding members of what was to be, in the years leading up to the Revolution, the most celebrated Masonic lodge in Paris: the Neuf Sœurs, named after the Muses. Parny joined as number 77, probably in 1777. Among its founders the lodge included Jean-François Cailhava (1731–1813) who was to become a prominent dramatist. Authors such as Louis-Sébastien Mercier or Nicolas Brimaire de La Dixmerie, as well as artists like Greuze and Vernet and scientists such as Montgolfier and J.-J. Le François de Lalande were also 'brothers'. The list of members reads like a *Who's Who* of the chattering classes in pre-Revolutionary France. It is said that on being initiated, candidates had to present a piece of work to the assembled company. Jacques Lemaire suggests that Parny's satirical piece on the American Revolution, the *Épître aux Bostoniens*, may have been the 'planche' he offered to the Lodge.[13] It is a slight poem which feigns to chide the Bostonians for claiming freedoms which Europeans did not enjoy. During the Revolution, Parny was to quote it as an indication of his precocious democratic leanings.

The regular meetings with like-minded individuals at the Loge des Neuf Sœurs must have proved intellectually stimulating. They also ensured that Parny had a social circle to hand and an appreciative audience in 1778 when he published his first collection of verse, which followed on the heels of selected individual poems printed at the end of 1776 and of 1777 in a renowned periodical, the *Almanach des Muses*.[14] On 14 February 1778, the *Catalogue hebdomadaire des Livres mis en vente* listed Parny's *Poésies érotiques* among the newly published books. The title uses 'erotic' in the sense of relating to love and indicates a debt to Latin poets such as Tibullus, Catullus or Propertius. The slim 64-page volume contains a number of poems, mostly, but by no means all, dedicated to Éléonore. They are pleasant to read and were to spark off a revolution far greater than their inspiration would seem to indicate. The success of this poetry[15] was in part due to a publicity machine which aimed at finding a young champion to counter Claude-Joseph Dorat (1734–1780), whose star was waning. It was also to be an encouragement to a talented young poet who subsequently revised his book completely and turned it into a truly original and moving work. A few weeks after the initial publication, the Neuf Sœurs sent a deputation to pay homage to the dying Voltaire on his return to Paris, and legend says that the great author, on being introduced to the young Parny, addressed him as 'Mon cher Tibulle'. Whether fact or fiction, this encounter between the elder statesman of French literature and one of its rising stars was used to great effect. Parny was to be known thereafter as 'Le Tibulle français'. Fame brought other rewards such as a captaincy in the Dragoons.

Considerably revised, the 1781 edition of the *Poésies érotiques* is divided into four books which tell the tale of a doomed love-affair between the narrator and Éléonore. In the first, the poet narrates the birth of the relationship. The second tells of a tiff. The third celebrates renewed ties between the lovers. The fourth, entirely made up of elegies, is a poignant cry of pain after separation which was to mark the elegy, forever after in France, as a poem of memory and regret. The structure of the *Poésies érotiques* is not unlike a sonata form with echoes from one book to another. Young readers were bowled over. Chateaubriand recounts that he knew the poems by heart.[16] He was not alone. Many contemporaries felt that an aesthetic revolution was under way. Ginguené recalls it thus:

> L'Esprit et l'art avaient proscrit le sentiment;
> L'ironique jargon, l'indécent persiflage
> Prenaient, en grimaçant, le nom de bel usage.
> Le bel-esprit est mort, son empire est fini.
> Qui donc l'a détrôné? La nature et Parny.[17]

In 1782, another aspiring writer, Félix-François Nogaret, published a pamphlet celebrating the author under the title *Lettre et monologue d'un jaloux sur les opuscules de Monsieur le chevalier de Parny*. The simplicity of the author's style, his brief poems and apparently directly expressed feelings charmed his contemporaries. His success was greater than that of another talented poet who was a close friend, Antoine de Bertin, whose *Amours* first came out in 1780. Interestingly enough, Bertin, like Parny and other gifted writers of the time such as Michel-Paul Gui de Chabanon (1730–1792) and Nicolas-Germain Léonard (1744–1793), was born in the colonies. It is as though the renewal of French verse was rendered possible by the otherness which these men must have felt, and by their knowledge, however superficial, of other lands and languages. Romantic poets such as Lamartine and Musset owe a considerable – but rarely recognized – debt to the *Poésies érotiques*.

Over the years, Parny was to publish various other texts, essentially poems, but also a version of his travel journal written on the way back to Bourbon. His next major step in literature came in 1787 after another trip to his homeland where he went to settle the family's affairs after his father's death. He travelled in an official capacity, almost certainly to save money, and ended up going to Ceylon and India with the vicomte de Souillac. The trip had hardly any impact on his inspiration. There are a few rapid allusions to it in a verse epistle called *À mon frère*, and the later *Voyages de Céline* include a nodding reference to suttee. Parny was obviously missing France and his friends. His observations on the unfairness of society in Asia may have been indirectly responsible for his added attention to the fate of the Malagasy population as would become apparent in texts published on his return to Paris.

After a brief stop in London where he was to communicate with the French Ambassador, Parny met up with his nephew, Geneviève's son, who was hale and hearty, and with Jean-Baptiste who had been dangerously ill.[18] Back in Paris he asked to be allowed the *Honneurs de la Cour*, often a necessary prelude to seeking a wealthy match, and was admitted on 26 October 1786, his name-day. He subsequently assumed the courtesy title of 'vicomte de Parny',[19] Jean-Baptiste, his elder brother, being known as the 'comte de Parny'. He must also have had dealings with the literary world as Hardouin and Gattey published his *Chansons madécasses traduites en français suivies de Poésies fugitives* in March 1787. The twelve prose poems which open the volume and give it its title are said to be translations of Malagasy originals. The choice not to use verse seems to afford Parny's inspiration a form of liberation which taps into the primitive trend launched by 'Ossian' but also includes references to some Malagasy names and traditions. He depicts Madagascar not as a tropical paradise in a golden age, but as a society whose equilibrium was compromised by the arrival of the Europeans. On the whole, reception in the press was positive, though some critics preferred the more traditional verse poems included in the second part of the book.

Jean-Baptiste may never have fully recovered from the bout of illness he suffered during Parny's absence. We know he had occasion to call upon the services of Malouet who was the doctor by appointment to *Mesdames*, the King's aunts. Though he had resigned as equerry by 1784 and was, apparently, in straitened financial circumstances, the 'comte de Parny' had maintained contacts at Court. In August 1787 he went to stay in Croissy, outside Paris, at a house rented by Pierre-Dominique Bertholet-Campan, father-in-law to Marie-Antoinette's lady-in-waiting Madame Campan. Late at night on 15 August or early the next morning, Jean-Baptiste died from a 'fièvre maligne-nerveuse', an unidentifiable ailment. He was buried in Croissy at 9 p.m. as a local doctor, Lappoujade, from Rueil, feared contagion, which may suggest that typhoid or another such disease was to blame. Bertholet-Campan, his host, the Queen's 'Secrétaire de Cabinet', a neighbour, Antoine-Richard Travers de Beauvert, 'commissaire des guerres', and various members of the parish attended the funeral. Parny was apparently with his brother when he died but set straight off for Paris thereafter. He wrote movingly to family and friends on the loss of his closest relative as here in a letter to his nephew:

> Pleure, mon cher Duportail; pleure toutes les larmes de ton corps, ton oncle est mort avant-hier à Croissy d'une fièvre maligne-nerveuse, fais part de cette affreuse nouvelle à Mesdames de l'Isle, elles perdent un bon ami, tu perds beaucoup, et moi je perds tout, adieu, je te défends de me venir voir dans ce moment-ci.[20]

The poet renounced his share in his brother's succession as the debts outweighed the dead man's scanty possessions which included 38 shirts but only 25 volumes valued at 6 *livres*.[21] He also lost the money he had loaned to Jean-Baptiste. As a matter of honour he decided to pay the tradesmen, doctor, apothecary and other professional people with whom his brother had had a slate. Parny's losses were great, on a financial, a social, and a personal level. Jean-Baptiste had been closer to him than any friend. In many ways, the poet seems to have believed that his life, too, was at an end. To Geneviève he wrote that their two elder half-brothers and Jean-Baptiste having all died within a period of eighteen months, 'C'est maintenant mon tour, et je l'attends sans crainte. Je sais trop que ceux qui meurent ne sont pas les plus à plaindre'.[22] His two other great friends, Auguste Pinczon du Sel and Antoine de Bertin, were soon to leave France and die far from its shores.[23] So, believing himself to be living, in a sense, on borrowed time and, as such, probably never expecting to write again, Parny prepared an edition of his works which came out in 1788 under the title *Œuvres complètes*. His regiment was dissolved at around the same time and he seems to have withdrawn from society. A young Breton tells of his meeting with a prematurely aged, polite, but distant man:

> Je savais par cœur les élégies du chevalier de Parny, et je les sais encore. Je lui écrivis pour lui demander la permission de voir un poète dont les ouvrages faisaient mes délices; il me répondit poliment; je me rendis chez lui rue de Cléry.
>
> Je trouvai un homme assez jeune encore, de très bon ton, grand, maigre, le visage marqué de la petite vérole. Il me rendit ma visite; je le présentai à mes sœurs. Il aimait peu la société [...][24]

The visitor was Chateaubriand, for whom Parny was a senior figure in literature, a guide to whom aspiring writers could turn for advice. But as the portrait shows, Parny was no longer a carefree man about town. The Revolution must only have increased his tendency to melancholy. On various occasions, he considered returning to the tropics to be near his sister, but this was not to be. He may well have been unable to withdraw the funds he had invested, and he seems to have spent much of the revolutionary period in financial difficulties. In the letters he sent to Geneviève he complains of his lack of funds and generally sounds morose. His life was to become even more uncomfortable when he was listed as a suspect for the *Brutus* section in April 1794. Research in the revolutionary archives shows that his name was entered in error: his nephew Paul-Marie-Claude, the 'marquis de Parny', should have figured in his place as a friend of Théodore de Marsan, one of the royalists who had plotted to free Louis XVI on his way to the guillotine on the morning of 21 January 1793. The revolutionary tribunal would have been unlikely to take such niceties into account, so Parny chose the only sensible option and fled Paris. From Clichy, on 5 May, he wrote to the Comité de Salut Public to state his innocence and remind them of three lines of his *Épître aux Insurgents*, addressed to the American revolutionaries, which he brandishes as a guarantee of true republican sentiments:

> Sans pape, sans roi et sans reines,
> Vous danseriez au bruit des chaînes
> Qui pèsent sur le genre humain.[25]

Fortunately, the Terror ended shortly afterwards, but a number of Parny's friends and acquaintances had mounted the scaffold. In the meantime, to assure the revolutionary regime of his goodwill, the poet had taken up a challenge set by Bertrand Barère: for painters, sculptors and poets to celebrate the heroic crew of the *Vengeur*. His

80-line poem, unlike the one written by Ponce-Denis Écouchard Le Brun on the same event, is not a distant celebration of heroism but a text which shows the actions of the seamen and uses their vocabulary. It was published in the *Journal de Paris* on 1 Thermidor an II (19 July 1794), and though the author subsequently disowned the printed version, claiming a third of the lines were not his, the original autograph manuscript held in the Archives Nationales is identical to the published text.[26] Parny had sought inspiration in current events because his life was in danger. In many ways this new departure explains some of his subsequent works. His life in the shadow of noble families must have meant he felt some sympathy with democratic ideals. His difficult relationship with the Catholic Church can hardly have led him to regret its suppression. He was in many ways a disciple of the *philosophes*. Whilst the Revolution made a difficult financial situation worse, it also enabled his future wife, Grâce Vally, to divorce. It consecrated the death of one strain of inspiration: Parny would no longer be the intimate poet of young love. His verse would henceforth deal with ideas and seek a wider field.

One of the immediate effects of Parny's poem on the *Vengeur* was to allow him to be included by Marie-Joseph Chénier – the dramatist and brother of the then unknown poet, André Chénier, who was guillotined just before Robespierre was overthrown – on a list of deserving intellectuals to whom the Convention Nationale attributed funds. He received 2000 francs along with Restif de La Bretonne, Suvée, Lacretelle and Cailhava amongst others. The sum was not sufficient to resolve his financial problems. He sought gainful employment in an administrative capacity. Thanks to Ginguené, he was given clerical responsibilities in the Ministère de l'Intérieur along with other authors like Nogaret, Bouilly or Régnaud.[27] He seems to have found a new impetus to write. From 20 ventôse an III (10 March 1795), extracts from his work in progress, *La Guerre des Dieux anciens et modernes*, started to appear in the *Décade*, the paper run by the so-called *idéologues*, one of whom was none other than Ginguené. Parny appears to have found a trustworthy circle of friends who encouraged him to write a text which mocked Christianity on aesthetic grounds, claiming the pagan gods were far more attractive and interesting as mythological creations.

Probably in order to offer him better conditions to work on his mock epic, Ginguené suggested that Parny be given a position as one of the administrators of the Théâtre des Arts, the former Opera, along with Julien Mazade, La Chabeaussière and Caillot. Appointed on 1 Vendémiaire an V (3 June 1796), Parny resigned on 6 June 1797 in protest at the Ministry's asking for the theatre's funds to be handed over. His job seems to have been to read the plays which were submitted, to have some control over the repertoire and also, curiously, to rewrite various texts in order to make them politically correct for the new regime by editing any references to thrones, kings and all things monarchic. A furore erupted over his bowdlerized version of Gluck's *Alceste*.[28] He was, however, at the government's request, to carry out a similar task from home, verifying that literary masterpieces by the likes of Corneille, Racine or La Fontaine no longer bore traces of ideas contrary to 'la doctrine de la liberté et de la raison'.[29] He was duly paid for his efforts, though it was decided part way through that adding explanatory notes to school texts would be a better idea than rewriting them.

Parny was thus protected by the new regime which attempted to turn him into one of its official poets. He had never saluted kings, queens or princes; he was however to contribute a hymn for the official ceremonies of the French Republic. The regime had set up a new calendar; regular feast-days were set to replace Christmas, Easter and the other traditional religious holidays; provision was also made for private events such as births and marriages. On behalf of the government, François de Neufchâteau ordered a series of texts and melodies, one each for five occasions:

1° *L'Hymne de l'Hymen*, pour servir à la fête des époux et à la célébration des mariages dans les temples décadaires ;

2° *L'Hymne de la Naissance*, pour la présentation des enfants nouveau-nés devant l'officier public, et la célébration de l'anniversaire du jour de naissance dans les familles ;

3° *L'Hymne de la Jeunesse*, pour la fête du 10 germinal et pour servir aussi dans les écoles publiques ;

4° *L'Hymne de la Vieillesse*, pour servir à la fête des vieillards ;

5° *L'Hymne de la Mort*, pour servir dans les sépultures et dans la fête qui pourrait être instituée à nos aïeux.[30]

Ducis, Mahérault, Parny, Arnault and Legouvé were contacted in turn. Parny was thus entrusted with writing the hymn to youth. He accepted with alacrity and the text was finished within a week.[31] It is a sort of secular cantata with different solo voices and a chorus. Young people of both sexes render homage to the homeland and speak of their future as they envision it. According to the musicologist Constant Pierre, 'Par sa destination, cet hymne devait être simple et facile. Il est aimable et tout à fait charmant.'[32] It showcases civic duties like patriotism, virtue and so on. The style is simple and graceful in the main, though there is a brief expression of bellicose sentiment when the youth of France swears to hate the monarchic yoke. Cherubini, one of the great composers of the time, wrote the melody, in C major, for voices and an accompaniment of two clarinets, two horns (in C) and two bassoons, traditional Masonic instruments. The hymn duly served for the patriotic celebration of the festival of youth in March 1799.

One of Parny's major works was still to come. Financial assistance was afforded by the government to allow him to finish and publish his mock epic *La Guerre des Dieux anciens et modernes*, the most controversial of his poems. It is an amusing and irreverent text in which God is a tyrant, only interested in praise, and impervious to the disputes in Heaven where the Christians, briefly abetted by the Nordic pantheon, are trying to take over from the Gods of Greece and Rome. For Fernand Drujon it is a 'poème aussi élégant qu'impie et immoral'[33] while Colnet complained that Parny had 'prostitué [ses] pinceaux à d'indécentes priapées'.[34] Many people were shocked by what Labitte called 'Ce poème de Parny qu'on ne nomme pas'.[35] Nothing appears sacred, yet there are charming idyllic scenes of seduction, amusing passages in which fights break out, swipes at the Church's distribution of titles, but also, at the beginning of the third canto, a declaration of theism by a dead man arriving in Paradise which, with its defence of religious tolerance, may well state the author's own beliefs. Parny was certainly influenced by Voltaire's mock epic about Joan of Arc, *La Pucelle*. He was trying to accommodate the Voltairian tradition and the new regime, but his style is very much his own.

The book was an instant bestseller with reprints and forgeries. Many readers were scandalized that Parny was taking a shot at beliefs for which people had died just a few years earlier. The poem would have seemed an in-joke at Frederick of Prussia's table a few decades earlier, if we are to believe Sainte-Beuve.[36] It was deemed hurtful when published, in spite of a spirited defence by the *idéologues*, led by Ginguené, for whom 'Attaquer par des fictions ingénieuses ces religions positives ennemies du bonheur de l'homme, verser à flots le ridicule sur ce qui fit verser tant de sang, c'est bien mériter de la religion et de l'humanité.'[37] On 10 Vendémiaire the *Ami des Lois* stated that 'Tous les poètes réunis de l'Institut ne pourraient faire une page de la *Guerre des Dieux*.' The second edition toned down the more scandalous scenes which had been judged sacrilegious or licentious. The whole affair illustrates the discrepancy that there was between the intellectuals who dominated government positions and the grass-roots level where faith had remained solid despite recent history. It is worthy of note, for the literary historian, that Chateaubriand was moved to write his *Génie du Christianisme* as 'une sorte de réponse au poème du pauvre Parny, notre ancien ami qui vient de se déshonorer bien gratuitement'.[38] An enlarged version to be called *La Christianide* was never published and, indeed, probably never finished.

Parny's aim in writing *La Guerre des Dieux* and his subsequent *Paradis perdu* seems to have been to defend his views on religious toleration and not simply, as certain critics have claimed, to make money through verse. At the time, he was involved in a sort of lay church called Le Portique Républicain whose members met every ten days for philosophical and literary readings. In a letter to a young admirer, Auguste de Labouïsse, on 20 Prairial an XIII, he defended his attitude: 'Avec quelle légèreté les auteurs eux-mêmes lisent, jugent et condamnent les auteurs! Vous me reprochez l'athéisme, le matérialisme; et j'ai clairement énoncé dans mon poème la doctrine contraire, un Dieu, l'immortalité de l'âme, les peines et les récompenses futures. Les prêtres voudraient bien que je fusse athée; beaucoup d'autres me traitent de capucin.'[39]

Possibly in order to ride the tide of French nationalism against the hereditary enemy across the channel, Parny then published a slight but witty propaganda text in verse, *Goddam! Poème par un French-dog*. He may have been trying to reduce the negative impact of his *Guerre des Dieux*. He may also have recalled famous cases in which licentious poems had been used to exclude leading writers from that hallowed sanctuary of French letters, the Académie, which had been reformed after its suppression as a monarchic institution. Now known as the Institut National, it was divided into classes, the second of which was soon to be devoted to 'la langue et la littérature françaises'. After a lengthy press campaign, Parny was duly elected. His acceptance speech, read at a public assembly on 6 Nivôse an XII (28 December 1803), dealt with elegiac verse, an uncontroversial subject. Garat, who welcomed him, praised *La Guerre des Dieux*, much to the displeasure of the reactionary wing of the press at a time when Bonaparte was endeavouring to reconcile France and the Vatican. As a member of the Institut, Parny took his task seriously, contributing papers, writing articles for the *Dictionnaire* and involving himself in the electoral process.

Parny seems to have led a fairly settled life thereafter. On 25 Frimaire an XI, he married the woman with whom he had been living for some time, Marie-Françoise-*Grâce* Vally, born on 13 October 1756, like him on Bourbon, and divorced from Antoine Fortin since June 1794. We do not know whether they had known each other since childhood. It seems likely. They had certainly moved in the same circles for some years, since we have indications that they attended the same lunches and dinners during the Revolution. It has been suggested, though with no real evidence given, that Parny sired Grâce Vally's youngest child, Henri-Gédéon-*Eugène*, born on 4 January 1787.

The 'homme de lettres', as Parny was described on his marriage contract, seems to have found it difficult to satisfy his audience in his latter years. He had abandoned the short, light, love poetry which had made him famous in favour of longer, ideologically-marked verse. In 1805, he published a collection of three works: *Le Portefeuille volé*. The 246 pp. first edition was published by Debray, with some title-pages bearing the indication 'Magasin de librairie'.

The title *Le Portefeuille volé* is reminiscent of a collection of Voltaire's verse called *Le Portefeuille trouvé*. It harks back to the literary tradition of 'fugitive' poems being kept by the author in his 'portefeuille' and being stolen by an indiscreet friend who then publishes them without seeking the writer's permission. The anonymity of the collection contributed to the fiction of a clandestine publication. Parny never denied his authorship. Indeed he even sent copies of the volume to acquaintances like Héseque, his 'avoué'.[40] He presumably omitted his name on the title-page in order not to anger the Emperor.

The *Portefeuille volé* contains *Le Paradis perdu*, a poem in four cantos which is not without recalling the *Guerre des Dieux*; *Les Déguisements de Vénus*, a series of tableaux narrating scenes of the seduction of a shepherd, Myrtis, by the Goddess Venus, and *Les Galanteries de la Bible*, subtitled *Sermon en vers*, a set of libertine vignettes based on biblical stories, some of them well known, others quite forgotten, particularly in a country where sacred texts were rarely read by the public at large. All three works, in their way, were responses to the climate of pro-Catholic apologetic literature which was encouraged by the State. They presented Christianity as containing its fair share of violent and lewd episodes in spite of what the ten commandments dictate.

A year later, *Les Voyages de Céline* showed a woman betrayed by her husband touring the world in order to try and find an ideal place to live. From the United States to New Zealand, China, Tartary, Ceylon, Southern Africa, etc., nowhere meets her expectations. Life may be difficult for women in France, the poem concludes, but they could well be worse off elsewhere —and, as a final concetto recalls, the Church had long maintained that they did not have souls, even though they are the most lovely of creatures. Parny was probably aiming at a female readership. The work is unpretentious but pleasing though without the emotional impact of the *Poésies érotiques* and *Chansons madécasses*.

Everything seems to indicate that Parny's gift was for shorter texts and amorous inspiration. His two best collections act at once as individual pieces and ensembles in which the whole is greater than the sum of its exquisite parts. In the longer works there are delightful episodes, but often the seams between them are too obvious. Boredom is more likely to set in when reading a single long poem than a series of shorter ones. Nowhere is this more true than in Parny's last work, *Les Rosecroix*, a woolly epic whose title refers to a decoration awarded by the heroine to trusty knights, but also possibly to the rank the author then occupied in the reformed Masonic Lodge of the Neuf Soeurs.[41] The poem, in twelve cantos, is dedicated to Français de Nantes, a friend and patron. There are nearly 100 characters and, as certain critics remarked on its publication, it is at times difficult to follow the plot. It takes place in the Middle Ages, in London, where English and French fight side by side against the Danes. Elfride, the young widow of a French prince, reigns in England. The text sets the high-minded Anglo-French characters against the treacherous Scandinavians. There are echoes of Tasso with a passage concerning an enchanted wood and various sub-plots involving the love of valorous soldiers and charming princesses. The poem ends with a plea for peace, loose ends having been tied, conquerors rewarded and lovers united. Harol [*sic*], who has lost the battle, accepts a new life as a gentleman farmer in East Anglia, all for the love of the beautiful Isaure. The decasyllabic verse and monotonous rhyme scheme were condemned by certain readers though others remarked upon interesting passages. The final line, offering an apparent reconciliation with Christianity, is a joyous cry: 'Vivent la rose, et la reine, et la croix.' The condemnation of war would have struck a chord with contemporary readers, who knew the true cost of Napoleon's campaigns, as would the poet's claim that 'Les vrais héros ne sont point conquérants'. In many ways the work has a conciliatory tone more evident than in Parny's other long works. Love redeems and humanity saves. Though it avoided criticizing the Church and contained no passages which could possibly be construed as lewd, the text was not particularly well received. In spite of its medieval décor, it could not rival Gothic novels, and many of its scenes fall flat. Its Manichean presentation of Good and Evil meant that the characters seemed to represent ideas rather than individuals.

Les Rosecroix was to be Parny's last book. He spent the final years of his life in poor health, perhaps as the result of a tropical disease.[42] Various friends managed to have him appointed to theoretical clerical jobs in ministries, though it appears that he received his salary without being required to do anything in return. He died without receiving the holy sacraments, in spite of his doctor's best endeavours to get him to agree to see a priest. He was buried at the Père-Lachaise cemetery on 7 December 1814, in the presence of ten members of the Academy and after a funeral mass at Notre-Dame de Bonne-Nouvelle. Étienne read a funeral oration over his tomb. Before the Revolution, the poet had written his own mock epitaph:

> Ici gît qui toujours douta,
> Dieu par lui fut mis en problème
> Il douta de son être même
> Mais de douter, il s'ennuya:
> Et las de cette nuit profonde,
> Hier au soir, il est parti,
> Pour aller voir en l'autre monde
> Ce qu'il faut croire en celui-ci.

Both Béranger[43] and Lamartine, amongst others, wrote poems deploring Parny's death and the famous writer was widely mourned in spite of the turbulent political situation in France.

Parny's posthumous reputation

Although Parny is now arguably known only to specialists in eighteenth-century French literature, he was in his day a renowned and widely-read author, referred to by Victor Hugo, George Sand and Balzac. Baudelaire described himself in 1846 as a 'poète qui veut marcher sur les traces d'un Pétrarque ou d'un Parny'[44] while Proust makes him the emblem of Ancien Régime elegance in the mind of a rich American woman whose sole – and unread – book is a volume of Parny's verse which she displays as it is 'du temps'.[45] There were many editions of his works throughout the nineteenth century. He was celebrated first and foremost for his love poetry, in particular the *Poésies érotiques* which many great writers like Chateaubriand and Lamartine claimed to know by heart, and which constituted a major influence not only on French, but also on Russian literature of the early nineteenth century,[46] as Anna Akhmatova's poetic description of the young Pushkin at Tsarskoe Selo shows.[47] He was also famous for his anticlerical verse – so much so that Hegel, in his lectures on aesthetics, used one of Parny's major poems, alongside verse by Goethe and Schiller, to illustrate the transition from paganism to Christianity:

> In another way, Parny, called the French Tibullus on the strength of his successful Elegies, turned against Christianity in a lengthy poem in ten books, a sort of epic, *La guerre des Dieux*, in order to make fun of Christian ideas by joking and jesting with an obvious frivolity of wit, yet with good humour and spirit. But these pleasantries went no further than frolicsome levity, and moral depravity was not made into something sacred and of the highest excellence as it was at the time of Friedrich von Schlegel's *Lucinde*. Mary of course comes off very badly in Parny's poem; monks, Dominicans, Franciscans, etc. are seduced by wine and Bacchantes, and nuns by fauns, and thus it goes on perversely enough. But finally the gods of the Greek world are conquered and they withdraw from Olympus to Parnassus.[48]

Parny's cosmic satires remained current throughout the nineteenth century among libertine and anticlerical writers. Heine's depictions of the supersession of paganism by Christianity, notably the famous passage in his *History of Religion and Philosophy in Germany* in which Kant is described as storming Heaven and assassinating God, were recognized as showing the influence of Parny.[49] Pushkin, who includes some flattering references to Parny's erotic verse in *Eugene Onegin*,[50] drew on *La Guerre des Dieux* for the even more scabrous *Gavriliiad*, in which the sixteen-year-old Mary feels worn out after enjoying the Archangel Gabriel, Satan (as a serpent), and God (as a dove), all in one day.[51] In *Madame Bovary*, Flaubert makes Charles Bovary's anticlerical father spoil the mood of the christening feast by reciting passages from *La Guerre des Dieux*.[52] And as late as 1895, when the anticlerical writer Oskar Panizza was put on trial in Catholic Munich for his blasphemous drama *Das Liebeskonzil* (The Council of Love), in which a decrepit God punishes the debauchery of Renaissance Italy by creating a *femme fatale* to infect humanity with syphilis, he defended himself by citing Parny's poem as a reputable precedent for satirizing the Trinity.[53]

Although *La Guerre des Dieux* has recently become available in a scholarly edition, Parny's other main cosmic satire, his parody of *Paradise Lost*, remains in obscurity. Yet *Le Paradis perdu* amply deserves to be recovered, read, and enjoyed. It is, in the first place, a brilliantly witty satire. In its deft handling of decasyllables, the traditional metre for French burlesque verse, it owes much to Voltaire's *La Pucelle*. And as a humorous critique of Milton, it touches on many of the issues which have caused controversy in Milton criticism from the eighteenth century onwards, especially in the Milton wars of the mid twentieth century. For this reason it merits particular attention from Milton scholars concerned with the reception of *Paradise Lost*.

Many other works by Parny are also worthy of modern editions. As critics or authors occasionally recall, Parny was, without a doubt, one of the foremost poets of his time. His verse is hard to find nowadays: it is absent from school textbooks and, apart from the recent edition of *La Guerre des Dieux* and a more confidential one of the *Poésies érotiques*, it is only present in the pages of anthologies. He was, however, influential in the simplification of French poetic language which the Romantics were to claim as their own. At its best, Parny's poetry has an immediate quality which can touch the reader even today, ringing true and coming to life on the page.

The Reception of Milton in Eighteenth-Century France

Any account of Milton's reception does well to follow the understanding of *Paradise Lost* announced in Lucy Newlyn's study of its impact on the English Romantics: 'The poem is so rich in ambiguities, so resolute in highlighting the reader's role in construing their meaning, that it goes on provoking widely discrepant ideological interpretations.'[54] The word 'ideological' deserves a moment's attention. It has long been a commonplace that any ideology is put to a severe test when embodied in a work of literature. No ideology has all the answers: there will always be strains, contradictions, fault-lines, which in a discursive exposition can be glossed over or seemingly argued away, but which become visible when a great writer casts the ideology into narrative or dramatic form and asks how it plays itself out in actual human life.

In this sense, it is not unjust to call the Christianity of *Paradise Lost* an ideology. With its two heterogeneous and often discordant sacred books, supplemented by a prodigious wealth of theological elaboration, Christianity, in whatever version, is a hugely complex system of ideas, held at best in precarious suspension. When it is given dramatic or narrative form, as it is by Milton, the diverse elements start to fall apart, the links that were barely managing to hold them together become loose, and the tensions in the system become impossible to ignore. To claim that in *Paradise Lost* the theoretical claims of Christianity are tested against actual human life may sound paradoxical, since so many of the actors are divine or angelic, but such beings have to be given not only human speech but human qualities in order to be intelligible.

The abstract claims of Christian principles are set against their embodiment in action, in an intensely vivid realization of the Christian myth. Hence a major issue in the famously contested history of Milton's reception concerns the discrepancies between what he says and what he shows, between theological statement and dramatic action. Two of the standard reference points in twentieth-century Milton criticism will illustrate this issue. A.J.A. Waldock, in '*Paradise Lost*' *and the Critics* (1947), pointed out Milton's habit of first showing us behaviour that is in some way attractive or even admirable, then inserting comments that invite us to disapprove of it. Thus the famous opening speech in which Satan expresses his continuing defiance of heaven is followed by the information that while he spoke these 'vaunting' words he was really 'racked with deep despair' (*PL* i. 126).[55] Or, when Adam realizes what Eve has done and that he cannot bear not to share her punishment, Waldock says, surely rightly, that Adam's Fall is motivated by his love for Eve.[56] Yet Milton promptly explains that Adam was 'fondly overcome with female charm' (*PL*

ix. 999). It would seem then that the poem repeatedly invites two readings: one that appreciates human qualities (even in non-human beings) and responds with a measure of sympathy; and another that withdraws the sympathy on theological grounds. There is a constant uneasy process of reinterpretation: Satan's fortitude is quickly interpreted as bravado, Adam's love as 'uxoriousness' (the word used by C.S. Lewis).[57] How then are we to read the poem? Are we to accept a conflict, perhaps resulting from Milton's divided impulses, between (for want of a better shorthand) humanism and theology? Or are we to persuade ourselves that the human qualities are not there in the poem, but are a mere illusion generated by anachronistic readings, and that the careful reconstruction of Milton's theology can dispel them?

It was by seeming to accept *both* alternatives that Stanley Fish's *Surprised by Sin* (1967) became another reference point in Milton studies.[58] The humanist interpretation, Fish asserted, was perfectly legitimate, and Milton was deliberately inviting it. But Milton was doing so in order to educate the reader, who would first yield to an impulse of sympathy for Satan or Adam, then be made to realize his error by the orthodox theological interpretation which Milton had carefully inserted just afterwards. On the face of it, this seemed to solve all interpretative problems and to reconcile all Milton's readers. Present-minded critics who stuck to the words on the page were right, but so were historically-minded scholars who sought to reconstruct past meanings. However, there was a catch. Fish assumed that Christian theology was a closed intellectual world, within which there could be no disagreement, only misunderstanding. The reader was placed in the position of a pupil who had to learn how to discipline his emotions and accept the iron rule of theological orthodoxy. According to Fish, the technique he had identified in Milton was a standard method of Christian didacticism; but this claim only confirms that Fish's reading deserves to be called 'authoritarian' (Newlyn, p. 10). It also implied that *Paradise Lost*, like a textbook, could only be read once. On a second reading, one would be aware of the traps Milton was setting; one would no longer be tempted to sympathize with Satan or Adam; one would have outgrown the poem.

In sketching the eighteenth-century reception of Milton as the background to Parny's parody, it will be assumed that – although the debate on Milton has of course moved on – Waldock is a more reliable guide to the poem's effects than Fish, and that *Paradise Lost* is, as Newlyn says, indeterminate, inviting and permitting a wide variety of responses and interpretations.

Eighteenth-century France was unpromising soil for the reception of *Paradise Lost*. Knowledge of English was still so rare that Milton was more likely to be known through the Latin verse translation of *Paradise Lost, Paradise Regained*, and *Samson Agonistes* published as *Paraphrasis poetica* by the Scottish Latinist William Hogg in 1690.[59] Eventual French translations were unreliable. The first were in prose. In 1729 Nicolas Dupré de Saint-Maur published anonymously a version which aroused wide attention, reaching its seventh edition by 1740. Louis Racine was so impressed by it that he learnt English in order to read Milton in the original, but having done so, he perceived the inaccuracy of Saint-Maur's translation and undertook his own, also in prose. Jean-Baptiste Mosneron, considering Racine's version accurate but extremely dull, offered his own prose translation in 1786. Meanwhile, in 1748, Madame Du Bocage published a verse imitation called *Le Paradis terrestre*, preceded by eight lines of verse 'À Milton', addressed to the 'Homère des Anglais'. The first complete translation into verse was by the Abbé Leroy in 1775, followed in 1777 by another by one Beaulaton. Both were badly received, and were superseded by the verse translation by Jacques Delille, published in 1805.[60]

These translators took remarkable liberties. Although they admired the sublimity of the poem, they were annoyed by undignified details such as Satan's transformation of himself into a toad. Hence Delille, instead of using the obvious word 'crapaud', substitutes 'reptile' (Gillet, p. 506). Most also took exception to Milton's Protestantism and to his unusual version of Protestant theology. Like Newton and Locke, Milton was an Arian, who rejected the doctrine of the Trinity. From the text of the Bible, he argues in *On Christine Doctrine* that the Son, unlike the Father, cannot have existed from all eternity, but must have been begotten by the Father at some point in time before the Creation; and, though begotten from the divine substance, he cannot be of the same essence as his Father.[61] Although the question of Milton's heresy has been a source of dispute among twentieth-century Milton scholars, many of whom prefer to interpret his theology as orthodox, his Arianism was noticed by many British readers in the eighteenth century.[62] It was also picked up in France. Thus his opening description of Christ as a 'greater man' (*PL* i. 4) seemed shocking confirmation of his anti-trinitarianism. So Mosneron corrects his theology by translating this as 'homme-dieu' (Gillet, p. 531). The devout Catholic Leroy removes all references to classical mythology, considering them unsuitable for a Christian epic (Gillet, p. 358), while the *philosophe* Beaulaton keeps the classical mythology but reduces the biblical references (Gillet, pp. 361–62). Delille, disapproving of Milton's attack on priestly celibacy, introduces into the hymn to married love a eulogy of priests for their virtue in renouncing it (Gillet, p. 506). Unless, like Voltaire, one could read Milton in the original, one therefore had limited and unreliable access to the poem.

Those who could appreciate *Paradise Lost* – sometimes with the aid of Addison's admiring essays published in the *Spectator* – duly praised its sublimity, as Voltaire did (admittedly in an essay written initially for English readers):

> The Meanness (if there is any) of some Parts of the Subject is lost in the Immensity of the Poetical Invention. There is something above the reach of human Forces to have attempted the Creation without Bombast, to have describ'd the Gluttony and Curiosity of a Woman without Flatness, to have brought Probability and Reason amidst the Hurry of imaginary Things belonging to another World, and as far removed from the Limits of our Notions as they are from our Earth.[63]

When Voltaire published the French version of this essay in 1733, however, he was considerably more critical of Milton, emphasizing the elements he found incoherent or absurd. This may be, as David Williams suggests, because the success of Dupré de Saint-Maur's translation had reduced Voltaire's standing as the introducer of Milton into France, and threatened to overshadow his own epic, the *Henriade*.[64]

There were, however, major difficulties in accepting the Christian epic as a valid genre. Such poems ran counter to the widespread view that 'le merveilleux chrétien' was unsuitable for poetry. Torquato Tasso, who celebrated the First Crusade in his *Gerusalemme Liberata*, had claimed that the Christian supernatural could offer an adequate substitute for the outmoded gods of classical epic:

> The poet ought to attribute actions that far exceed human power to God, to his angels, to demons, or to those granted power by God or by demons, for example, saints, wizards, and fairies. Such actions, if considered in themselves, will seem marvellous; nay, they are commonly called miracles. But if

regarded in terms of their agent's efficacy and power, they will seem verisimilar.⁶⁵

This solution allowed Tasso to introduce into his epic such inventions as the infernal council, the enchanted forest created by the sorcerer Ismeno, and the voyage to Armida's island where she holds Rinaldo in her sexual thrall. Some commentators thought Milton similarly successful. Thus the Abbé Conti, who not only knew *Paradise Lost* in the original but had also read Addison's essays on its beauties, praised Milton's War in Heaven as superior to the classical myth of the war between Zeus and the giants, and the allegorical figures of Chaos, Sin, and Death as more terrifying than the denizens of Hades (Gillet, p. 23).

But the substitution of the Christian for the classical supernatural did not satisfy everyone. Even some authors of biblical epics were half-hearted. They were so steeped in classical mythology, and so fond of it, that they kept smuggling it in: thus Milton falls into a wistful tone when recounting how Hephaestus was thrown out of heaven and fell for nine days before landing on Lemnos, and French poets are equally nostalgic.⁶⁶ Boileau is in no doubt that the 'merveilleux chrétien' is intolerable: it degrades the mysteries of Christianity, and its effect is either tedious or ridiculous:

> Et quel objet enfin à présenter aux yeux,
> Que le Diable toûjours heurlant contre les Cieux [...]?⁶⁷

Voltaire predictably came down against the Christian epic. In his *Essay on Epick Poetry*, he maintains that modern taste rejects supernatural beings, whether Christian or classical, in epic:

> The antient Gods are exploded out of the World. The present Religion cannot succeed them among us. The Cherub, and the Seraph, which act so noble a Part in Milton, would find it very hard to work their way into a French Poem. The very Words of Gabriel, Michael, Raphael, would run a great Hazard of being made a Jest off. Our Saints who make so good a Figure in our Churches, make a very sorry one in our Epick Poems. St. Denis, St. Christopher, St. Rock, and St. Genevieve, ought to appear in Print no where, but in our Prayer-Books, and in the History of the Saints (iiiB. 394).

The article 'Merveilleux' in the *Encyclopédie*, which follows closely the authority of Boileau and Voltaire, deplores the Christian marvellous as deployed by Tasso, Camoens, and Milton. The last is rebuked for 'des fautes grossières et inexcusables', such as letting the devils build the palace of Pandaemonium which is not large enough for them all to fit in, so that most have to shrink to pygmies – something Voltaire had already ridiculed as 'preposterous' (iiiB: 381–82).[68]

God and Foreknowledge

Besides querying Milton's choice of genre, eighteenth-century French critics raised a number of the problems in *Paradise Lost* which have agitated Miltonists more recently. One is the presentation of God. It is widely agreed among modern commentators that Milton would have done better to keep God 'awful, mysterious and vague' (Lewis, p. 126). Such an oxymoron as 'Dark with excessive light thy skirts appear' (*PL* iii. 380) conveys God's majesty more impressively than any personification could. By giving the Supreme Being a dramatic presence, Milton inevitably endows him with a personality which is not always attractive and brings into relief the dubious aspects of his providential plans. William Empson may be extreme in calling him a 'jovial old ruffian'.[69] But many people have been unsatisfied by God's testy explanation that the Fall of Man is entirely Man's own fault:

> Whose fault?
> Whose but his own? Ingrate, he had of me
> All he could have: I made him just and right,
> Sufficient to have stood, through free to fall (*PL* iii. 96–99).

This self-justification may well be self-defeating. Marie-Anne Du Bocage (1710–1802) seems to have thought so. In her six-canto verse imitation, *Le Paradis terrestre*, dedicated to the Academicians at Rouen who two years earlier, in 1746, had awarded her a prize in their first-ever poetry competition, she took extensive liberties with the poem. They included the omission of the whole of Milton's Book III, with its theological reasoning. She maintains that even the *Iliad*, though much admired, has imperfections, and justifies her own amendments to *Paradise Lost* by referring to the 'hardiesse' of Pope's judgement that Milton was uneven, quoting his words in the original and in translation:

> Milton's strong pinions now not Heav'n can bound,
> Now serpent-like, in prose he sweeps the ground,
> In Quibbles, Angel and Archangel join,
> And God the Father turns a School-Divine.[70]

God's self-justification does not remove the awkward fact that all the deplorable events happen by God's permission. He suffers Satan to rise from the burning lake by 'the will | And high permission of all-ruling heaven' (*PL* i. 211–12), and 'permitted' the War in Heaven to last two days so that his Son could defeat the rebels on the third (*PL* vi. 674). Hell is locked, and Earth is guarded, but when these protections are really needed God allows them to be useless, and when Sin and Death reach earth, it is, God says, because 'I called and drew them thither' (*PL* x. 629). But if God is omnipotent, the distinction between letting things happen and making them happen is hard to sustain. Empson quotes a telling sentence from Aquinas:

> Knowledge, as knowledge, does not imply, indeed, causality; but, in so far as it is a knowledge belonging to the artist who forms, it stands in the relation of causality to that which is produced by his art.[71]

The problems of God's foreknowledge and responsibility were addressed by Pierre Bayle in various inconspicuous places in his *Dictionnaire*. Thus when ostensibly writing about a Manichaean sect, Bayle notoriously compared God's conduct to that of a mother who allowed her daughters to go to a ball while knowing in advance that they would succumb to temptation and lose their virginity there.[72] Not much credence need to be given to Voltaire's early praise of Milton's God: 'the God of Milton is always a Creator, a Father, and a Judge, nor is his Vengeance jarring with his Mercy, nor his Predetermination repugnant to the Liberty of Man' (3B:374–5). In the first version of his essay Voltaire intended to play off Milton's modern epic against the ancient epics which represent the gods as tyrannical. Even here, however, Voltaire also criticizes the inconsequence with which God first orders the archangels Michael and Gabriel to throw the rebels down to hell, then lets the war in Heaven rage for two days so that credit for victory can go to the Messiah (iiiB:386).

As for God's personality, Milton's God is capable of hate (his Son loyally says 'whom thou hat'st, I hate', *PL* vi. 734), and of 'anger infinite' (*PL* iv. 916); if 'incensed', he might respond by 'destruction' (*PL* viii. 235–36).[73] He shows sardonic humour, as when he pretends that the war in Heaven threatens his omnipotence (*PL* v. 721), to which his son dutifully replies: 'Mighty Father, thou thy foes | Justly hast in derision' (*PL* v. 735–36). Elsewhere it is predicted that human astronomy will evoke God's 'laughter' (*PL* viii. 78), and the Son teases Adam for wanting a companion when God needs none (*Pl* viii. 399–406).[74] Treating his subjects as imperiously as an eighteenth-century potentate, he sends his angels on futile missions 'for state, as sovereign king, and to inure | Our prompt obedience' (*PL* viii. 239–40). Gabriel implies that Heaven is an unpleasant place, full of obsequious flattery, when he says to Satan: 'who more than thou | Once fawned, and cringed, and servilely adored | Heaven's awful monarch?' (*PL* iv. 958–60). From this Empson concludes that 'God had already produced a very unattractive Heaven before Satan fell'.[75] And such a personality readily suggests the cantankerous and petulant tyrant of Parny's poem.

For the Enlightenment it was quite possible to reconceive the Christian God as an evil tyrant. Hume in his *Natural History of Religion* argued that primitive peoples may worship a being 'whom they confess to be wicked and detestable.'[76] As the idea of divinity develops, the notion of God's power increases, but not his goodness. Yet it is essential only to praise him, not to criticize him. 'The heart secretly detests such measures of cruel and implacable vengeance; but the judgment dares not but pronounce them perfect and adorable.'[77] Voltaire, responding to the Lisbon earthquake, could not but conjecture that God might after all be evil:

> De l'auteur de tout bien le mal est-il venu?
> Est-ce le noir Typhon, le barbare Arimane,
> Dont la loi tyrannique à souffrir nous condamne?[78]

Nicolas-Antoine Boulanger, an engineer who contributed five articles to the *Encyclopédie*, and whom Parny may have read, goes yet further in denouncing the Christian God as evil: 'Quant aux traits, sous lesquels Moyse a peint sa divinité, ni les Juifs, ni les Chrétiens, n'ont point droit de s'en glorifier. Nous ne voyons en lui qu'un despote bizarre, colere [*sic*], rempli de cruauté, d'injustice, de partialité, de malignité, dont la conduite doit jetter tout homme, qui le médite, dans la plus affreuse perplexité.'[79] The God of Christian epic was not, therefore, necessarily an improvement on the pagan divinities.

The crucial evidence that classical epic could not simply be converted into Christian epic was the difficulty of managing warfare, which was the staple of classical epic. Heroic combats made no sense if conducted by immortal supernatural beings under the aegis of an omnipotent God. Hence Milton's War in Heaven came in for persistent criticism. It requires spiritual beings to be shown fighting with material armour, swords, and guns. Some earlier poetic treatments, such as the twelfth-century prose epic by Rupert of Deutz, *De victoria Verbi Dei*, showed the Son defeating Satan with only spiritual weapons.[80] But such weapons cannot really be represented in poetry. Yet the use of material weapons is rendered absurd by the fact that both sides are immortal and cannot be killed, no matter what weapons they wield. Samuel Johnson drew the blunt conclusion that these absurdities must spoil the episode for adult readers: 'The confusion of spirit and matter which pervades the whole narration of the war of heaven fills it with incongruity; and the book, in which it is related, is, I believe, the favourite of children, and gradually neglected as knowledge is increased.'[81] This may be unfair to Milton, who seems to have believed that angels were a class of beings intermediate between God and man, with both spiritual and corporeal qualities. When the archangel Raphael has lunch with Adam and Eve, he really eats and digests, 'with keen dispatch | Of real hunger, and concoctive heat | To transubstantiate' (*PL* v. 436–38). So Milton's angels may have needed their armour. But this does not dispose of the objection that their weaponry becomes grotesque. Voltaire, who considered the whole episode 'an injudicious Imitation of Homer' (iiiB:385), complained that 'Angels arm'd with Mountains in Heaven, resemble too much the Dipsodes in Rabelais, who wore an Armour of Portland Stone six Foot thick', and that in using the harmless artillery, the immortal beings were only playing at ninepins (iiiB:386).[82] In making his parody centre on the War in Heaven, therefore, Parny was using material that was ready made for his purposes.

Eighteenth-century critics anticipated their modern successors in finding fault with many minor features of *Paradise Lost*. Jean-François Marmontel, the author and literary theorist, who often quotes Milton when considering the virtues – or otherwise – of epic poetry, salutes the strong portrayal of Satan – 'qu'Homère lui aurait envié' – before giving a long list of alleged absurdities in his 'Essai sur le goût':

> Quoi de plus absurde et de plus monstrueux que cet amas de fictions dont il a chargé son poème? Et peut-on ne pas reconnaître les rêves de la barbarie dans la transformation de l'ange rebelle en crapaud, dans ce vilain amas d'accouplements incestueux de Satan avec le Péché, et du Péché avec la Mort, et dans l'atelier des démons fabriquant du canon pour foudroyer

les anges, et dans ces batailles où les démons sont cuirassés et où les anges sont pourfendus, etc., etc.[83]

The allegory of Sin and Death was much reprehended. Even Addison's eulogistic essays suggested that it was contrived and old-fashioned: 'Such Allegories rather savour of the Spirit of *Spencer* and *Ariosto*, than of *Homer* and *Virgil.*'[84] French readers complained of its indecency (Gillet, p. 136). Voltaire professed to be scandalized 'on the Account of its Foulness' (iiiB:383); in 1733 he called it 'cette dégoûtante et abominable histoire' (iiiB:489). Some objected that the allegory only worked in English, since in French Satan would have to copulate with 'Péché', a masculine noun (Gillet, p. 54). Another aspect of Milton's imagination, the concern with precision which made him not only elaborate an imaginary astronomy but go into details about the angels' digestive system and sexual practices, could only scandalize readers accustomed to neoclassical generalities (see Gillet, pp. 143, 233). Voltaire, in *Questions sur l'Encyclopédie*, is particularly harsh on Milton's account of angelic digestion and excretion, and takes exception to the domestic phrase 'No fear lest dinner cool' (*PL* v. 396), which he even quotes in English in case his readers should refuse to believe that Milton had written so vulgarly (Moland, xviii. 583).

Other eighteenth-century criticisms anticipate the zeal with which twentieth-century commentators have listed incongruities in the poem. It is not only modern critics such as T.S. Eliot, for example, who have noted the inconsistencies in Milton's description of hell.[85] Bernard Routh in 1731 considered that hell was depicted much too pleasantly, with the devils able to engage in field sports and philosophical discussions when they were supposed to be undergoing torments: 'Cette vie me paraît la plus jolie chose du monde, je connais plus qu'un mortel qu'une pareille compagnie n'effrayerait point trop, et qui ne se croirait pas si fort à plaindre, s'il était condamné à passer les longs jours de l'éternité avec des diables si tranquilles et de si bonne humeur.'[86] The same criticism could undoubtedly be levelled against Parny's paradisal hell, which recalls scenes from Watteau, is reminiscent of ancien régime court life and an epitome of the Enlightenment where Satan is the most charming of hosts. Routh's contemporary, Constantin de Magny, is displeased with Gabriel for selecting 'two strong and subtle spirits' (*PL* iv. 786), as if other angels were feeble and lazy.[87] Louis Racine dislikes the account of Uriel 'gliding through the even | On a sunbeam' (*PL* iv. 555–56): 'Il suppose qu'un ange, pour descendre du ciel dans le paradis terrestre, se coule rapidement sur un rayon de soleil.'[88]

Satan as Revolutionary

Eighteenth-century critics take part in the old debate about who is the hero of the poem. Adam was thought not to qualify, because he is not martial, and because 'the Hero in the *Paradise Lost* is unsuccessful, and by no means a Match for his Enemies'.[89] Addison concluded that the Messiah must be the hero, but Dryden started a much more popular tradition by attributing the heroic role to Satan.[90] Several French commentators agree. Bernard Routh speaks enthusiastically of how 'Satan l'indomptable, Satan jusqu'au fond de l'abîme où il est presque anéanti montre cette elévation de génie, ces qualités brillantes, cette fierté qui l'avaient rendu le rival de Dieu même et asservi la moitié du Ciel à son Empire' (quoted in Gillet, p. 139). Here Routh even exaggerates Satan's achievement, since it was only a 'third part' of the heavenly host that Satan seduced (*PL* v. 710). Marmontel is another staunch supporter of the character and greatly admires the talent of the author who imagined him: 'Il fallait être Satan lui-même par la pensée, pour inventer son imprécation au soleil; il fallait le voir comme réellement sortir de l'abîme enflammé, pour le peindre *élevant son front cicatrisé par la foudre*.'[91] Similarly in Britain, Robert Burns told a correspondent in 1787 that he always carried a pocket Milton 'in order to study the sentiments – the dauntless magnanimity, the intrepid, unyielding independence; the desperate daring, and noble defiance of hardship, in that great Personage, Satan'.[92] And William Blake claimed that Milton was 'of the Devil's party without knowing it'.[93]

The reception of *Paradise Lost* was inevitably coloured by knowledge of Milton's republicanism. It was notorious that Milton had defended the execution of Charles I and engaged in a vituperative controversy about it with the French scholar Salmasius (Claude Saumaise). The article 'Milton' in Bayle's *Dictionnaire* introduces its subject as 'fameux Apologiste du suplice de Charles I Roi d'Angleterre'.[94] Later editions added more information about Milton's political career. Voltaire's 1733 essay differs markedly from its English original by including a long and highly critical account of Milton's politics. Milton is portrayed as led into corruption by excessive devotion to a good cause: 'Il était né avec une passion extrême pour la liberté. […] Il entra même assez avant dans la faveur de Cromwell; et par une fatalité, qui n'est que trop commune, ce zèlé républicain fut le serviteur d'un tyran' (iiiB:482). Returning to *Paradise Lost* in *Questions sur l'Encyclopédie*, Voltaire now finds the poem pervaded by fanaticism: 'Il est aisé de reconnaître dans cet ouvrage, au milieu de ses beautés, je ne sais quel esprit de fanatisme et de férocité pédantesque qui dominait en Angleterre du temps de Cromwell, lorsque tous les Anglais avaient la Bible et le pistolet à la main' (Moland xviii. 586). Louis Racine was fascinated by the attachment to liberty shown by Milton, the 'indomptable républicain', but ambivalent about 'son zèle, ou plutôt son fanatisme pour la cause de la liberté' (quoted in Gillet, p. 225). Charles Delalot, a royalist writing in the *Mercure de France* in 1804, takes exception to Milton's words 'Amongst unequals no society', as a false opinion which ignores the evident fact that inequality is the very foundation of society (Gillet, p. 490).[95] The royalist translator Delille distanced himself from Milton in a poem which calls him 'Admirable poète et mauvais citoyen' (quoted in Gillet, p. 506).

It was some time, however, before readers took the next step and sought a connection between the poetic rebellion of Satan and the actual rebellion of the Parliamentary forces against Charles I. In England, John Toland had already in 1698 hinted at a political reading by claiming that the poem's 'chief design' was to 'display the different Effects of Liberty and Tyranny' (Newlyn, p. 35), and in 1763–64 a debate conducted in the *Morning Chronicle* cast Satan as rebellious spokesman for the political opposition (*ib.*). In Germany, the young Schiller, writing his drama of social and oedipal rebellion, *Die Räuber* (1781), interpreted Milton's Satan as a genius in revolt, making his robber chief Karl Moor remark to an accomplice: 'Ich weiß nicht, Moritz, ob du den Milton gelesen hast. – Jener der es nicht dulden konnte, daß einer über ihm war, und sich anmaßte den Allmächtigen vor seine Klinge zu fordern, war er nicht ein außerordentliches Genie?'[96] [I do not know, Moritz, if you have read Milton. He who could not endure anyone to be above him, and presumed to challenge the Almighty – was he not an extraordinary genius?]

It was the French Revolution, however, which induced many readers to see Satan as a political hero. In his treatise *Political Justice*, the egalitarian philosopher William Godwin considered Satan justified in rejecting 'that extreme inequality of rank and power which the creator assumed' (quoted in Newlyn, p. 102). Godwin's son-in-law Shelley made the best-known case for Satan, though less by exalting Satan's qualities than by disparaging God's:

> Milton's Devil as a moral being is as far superior to his God, as one who perseveres in some purpose which he has conceived to be excellent in spite of adversity and torture, is to one who in the cold security of undoubted triumph inflicts the most horrible revenge upon his enemy, not from any mistaken notion of inducing him to repent of a perseverance in enmity, but with the alleged design of exasperating him to deserve new torments.[97]

In France, the link between Milton, Satan, and revolution was made by Xavier de Maistre, a passionate admirer of the 'sublime aveugle d'Albion'. Though he opposed the French Revolution, and could not approve of Satan's being 'un vrai démocrate, non de ceux d'Athènes, mais de ceux de Paris', de Maistre testifies to Satan's noble qualities: 'j'avoue que la fermeté qu'il montre dans l'excès du malheur et la grandeur de son courage me forcent à l'admiration malgré moi'.[98] Gillet notes that Parny's parody does nothing to disparage Satan's heroism (p. 497).

How far Satan can fairly be considered to express Milton's political sympathies is a perhaps insoluble question. While acknowledging Satan's intelligence, fortitude, and courage, the poem also makes clear that he is a 'tyrant' and 'Sultan' who assumes 'royal state'. The presence of republican language in Satan's speeches may signal Milton's lingering attachment to 'the good old Cause', or his disillusionment with it.[99] The crucial point is the imaginative appropriation of Satan as a figure of rebellion against tyranny in the period of the French Revolution, and here Parny deserves to be placed alongside Shelley among the chief exponents of such a view. It would not be lasting. In the post-revolutionary period, as Mario Praz has famously shown, Milton's Satan helped to reinforce the figure of the 'fatal man' in Gothic fiction, a conservative genre which depicts the power of the past over the present.[100] We meet him again in the person of Balzac's Vautrin: 'Son regard était celui de l'archange déchu qui veut toujours la guerre.'[101] But Vautrin, although an arch-criminal, is no revolutionary: later he makes his peace with society by becoming chief of police.

The Fall

In his *Paradis perdu*, Parny was inspired by Adam and Eve's transgression in the Garden of Eden. By using the Bible as the basis for his poem, he was once again acting as an heir to Voltaire. He parodied the scene without being sacrilegious. Parny's version, unlike

Madame Du Bocage's 1748 adaptation of Milton's poem, *Le Paradis terrestre*, was not to be taken seriously as an epic of Christian fall and redemption, but rather an ironic take on a good story. Parny's Satan is still a revolutionary. The poem treats him seriously, reserving its satire for God and the angels, and to a lesser extent for Adam and Eve. He is a proponent of reason as well as freedom, addressing his followers as 'Vous, à l'honneur, à la raison fidèles, | De l'esclavage éternels ennemis'. When in Heaven, his offence was that he got bored with perpetually singing the praises of a tyrant, the usual occupation of its inhabitants if we are to believe the *Guerre des Dieux*; after being summoned twice by God (as though to the headmaster's study) for not taking part in plainchant, he told his followers: 'De ma raison dois-je abjurer l'usage? | Non, le néant plutôt que l'esclavage!'

Another devil, invented by Parny, demands attention. This is Ammos, who in the brief infernal debate appears as the antagonist to Moloch. He thus occupies the position held in *Paradise Lost* by Belial, the prudent devil who 'with words clothed in reason's garb' (*PL* ii. 226) advises his fellows to avoid provoking further punishment from God and surmises that hell will grow milder, or else they will get used to it and no longer mind its discomfort. Indeed, once Satan has left on his expedition, the remaining devils seem to entertain themselves quite happily, some in sports, others in military exercises, others in tearing up rocks and hills for their amusement; other more civilized devils engage in philosophical debate or recite poems about their own military exploits, while yet others set off to explore the underworld. This 'atmosphere of busy planning' (Waldock, p. 94) must have suggested to Parny that hell could be made habitable with the aid of modern science. Ammos, a chemist, proposes to extract the chemical elements from their surroundings, recombine them, and so shape a new environment. He thus works out the practical implications of the mechanistic and materialist philosophy of nature, cautiously suggested in the article 'Chaos' in the *Encyclopédie*:

> Un philosophe qui ose entreprendre d'expliquer par les seules lois du mouvement, la méchanique & même la premiere formation des choses, & qui dit, *donnez-moi de la matiere & du mouvement, & je ferai un monde*, doit démontrer auparavant (ce qui est facile) que l'existence & le mouvement ne sont point essentiels à la matiere; car sans cela, ce philosophe croyant mal-à-propos ne rien voir dans les merveilles de cet Univers

que le mouvement seul ait pû produire, est menacé de tomber dans l'athéisme.[102]

Thus, while some devils go off exploring, and others invent the art of the theatre, Ammos quietly works out the physical laws governing hell, and puts its material into a crucible. Satan, on returning to hell, finds it transformed. Ammos has created an artificial blue sky, illuminated by a lamp (*réverbère*); the volcanic energies of hell have been transformed into a continual firework display; at its base there are meadows with flocks of animals, and Ammos has even outdone the four rivers of Paradise (Gen. 2:10-14) by creating four streams which respectively consist of water, sugared milk, wine, and coffee. This artificial paradise, outdoing the biblical Promised Land flowing with milk and honey, illustrates the practical application of the reason which Satan upholds.

Parny departs from Milton most obviously in his interpretation of the Fall. He equates it with the discovery of sex. Before the Fall, Eve feels bored (as does Adam, though he does not admit it), but does not know what she is missing. Satan discovers they have no knowledge of sensual pleasures, which he judges to be very unfair. He decides to take on Eve and pretends to be God's emissary warning her about the rebel angels and their seductive powers.

While Adam is busy praying, Eve tastes the forbidden fruit and with it love, life and happiness. She feels sexual desire and is fascinated by the sight of animals coupling. Adam sees hell upon her lips but has never found her so attractive. He remains impervious to her charms whilst all around them succumb to sensual pleasures and Eve feels unrequited desire: 'Si mon époux garde son ignorance, / Que faire, hélas! De ma vaine science?' she sighs. Fortunately, Satan is at hand and duly obliges. Adam will be vanquished when, with a brotherly kiss, he actually tastes the apple on Eve's lips. Everything changes instantly for him: 'Il pense enfin, il sent, il vient de naître.'

When Adam swallows the juice from her mouth, he is transformed:

> Pour lui tout change; il prend un nouvel être ;
> Il pense enfin, il sent, il vient de naître.
> Il voit alors et compte les appas
> Qu'il méconnut; des yeux il les dévore.

God's wrath can do nothing to change things. The couple loses the garden but gains knowledge and, as Adam says, 'Perdre ainsi, c'est gagner'. This amends Milton inasmuch as for Milton the Fall is problematic: disastrous in its consequences, yet empty in itself. In *On Christian Doctrine* Milton insisted that since the unfallen Adam and Eve were naturally inclined to do good and avoid evil, God could only test their obedience by prohibiting an action that was in itself indifferent: 'It was necessary that one thing at least should be either forbidden or commanded, and above all something which was in itself neither good nor evil, so that man's obedience might in this way be made evident.'[103] The fruit has no special properties; its prohibition is arbitrary. Yet a little later in *On Christian Doctrine* we read with astonishment that eating the fruit was not only a heinous sin, but comprehended all other sins:

> Anyone who examines this sin carefully will admit, and rightly, that it was a most atrocious offence, and that it broke every part of the law. For what fault is there which man did not commit in committing this sin? He was to be condemned both for trusting Satan and for not trusting God; he was faithless, ungrateful, disobedient, greedy, uxorious; she, negligent of her husband's welfare; both of them committed theft, robbery with violence, murder against their children (i.e. the whole human race); each was sacrilegious and deceitful, cunningly aspiring to divinity although thoroughly unworthy of it, proud and arrogant.[104]

The anomaly whereby the Fall is both catastrophic and trivial is avoided by Parny. His equation of the Fall with the discovery of sex was a highly unorthodox viewpoint. It was proposed in the scandalous treatise by Adriaan Beverland, *De peccato originali* (1678).[105] No less an authority than St Augustine, however, maintained that Adam and Eve not only remained chaste before the Fall, but did not even have any strong feelings: they were 'not distressed by any agitations of the mind, nor pained by any disorders of the body'.[106] If they had had sex, they would have conceived descendants 'by an act of will, instead of by a lustful craving': Adam would have had entire control of his erections, and Eve might have been impregnated without losing her virginity.[107] This theory of a prelapsarian freedom from passion, however, raised the question of how Eve was able to want the apple if she did not feel desire, and Augustine was obliged to divide the Fall into two: an initial, moral Fall with the awakening of evil desires, and a second, practical Fall when these desires were realized. To the question of how evil desires originated in beings created good,

Augustine has no answer.[108] Milton, however, makes his Adam and Eve enjoy prelapsarian sex which is much better than the inferior equivalent they experience after the Fall.

A related innovation in Parny's narrative is that the main agent of temptation is not the serpent but a bird. The serpent makes only a brief appearance, coiled round the branch of the fatal tree, telling Eve that the forbidden fruit has enabled him to speak. Then a bird with rainbow plumage takes over, singing:

> Reine de ce séjour,
> Écoutez-moi; je suis l'oiseau d'amour.
> Vous êtes belle et vous versez des larmes?
> Belle, et vos jours s'usent dans la langueur?
> Goûtez ce fruit, et connaissez vos charmes;
> Goûtez l'amour, la vie, et le bonheur.

This bird comes not from Milton, but from Tasso's *Gerusalemme Liberata*. It is the bird with multi-coloured plumage and a purple bill that inhabits the garden of the sorceress Armida, where the hero Rinaldo is kept in thrall. The bird urges people to pluck the rose and enjoy love before it is too late:

> Cogliam la rosa in su 'l mattino adorno
> di questo dì, che tosto il seren perde;
> cogliam d'amor la rosa: amiamo or quando
> esser si puote riamato amando.[109]

> O gather then the rose while time thou has,
> Short is the day, done when it scant began,
> Gather the rose of loue, while yet thou mast
> Louing, be lou'd; embrasing, be embrast.[110]

The fruit of Parny's Tree corresponds to Tasso's rose. It arouses Eve's amorous desire. Adam, who is rather slow, takes a while to follow her lead, but once the juice of the fruit has touched his lips, it has the desired effect.

This allusion to Tasso is also a humorous subversion of the entire epic tradition. For a standard motif of epic is the hero's distraction from his military duties by the allure of sensual love. Achilles sulks in his tent because of a dispute over a slave-girl; Aeneas dallies with Dido, and has to be recalled by the gods to his task of founding Rome; Voltaire's Henri in the *Henriade* is nearly diverted from his mission by his affair with Gabrielle d'Estrée; and Tasso's Rinaldo, of course, is needed because without his aid the Crusaders will be unable to take Jerusalem. Instead of the military virtues advocated by the epic tradition, Parny is putting the case for hedonism.

Not only for hedonism, though, but also for humanism. The Satanic assault on Heaven fails when the divine forces bring out their ultimate weapon – sprinklers (aspergilla) with which they douse their assailants in holy water. Satan himself stands his ground long enough to shoot at God with a pistol which narrowly misses its mark but removes God's beard. Then he retreats, but without shame, because he has gained the victory that really counts:

> « Messieurs, dit-il, de fuir je rougis peu.
> J'ai retouché votre œuvre favorite:
> Malgré la foudre, et malgré l'eau bénite,
> Le premier homme est homme enfin; adieu. »

That is, by introducing Adam to the prohibited pleasures of sex, Satan has freed him from God's tutelage and made him a man, in both senses: a fully human being and an adult male. And in case this emphasis on 'homme' should sound too exclusively masculine, one can add that Parny has implicitly revalued the role of Eve. While in all previous versions of the Fall Eve was blamed for leading Adam astray by her curiosity and sensuality, here she actually guides Adam out of his child-like immaturity and into an adult existence enriched by 'Le don d'amour'.

Le Paradis perdu in its time

Le Paradis perdu contains references to recent history, not only in Satan's connections with the avant-garde of the Ancien Régime, but also with the 'bleus' who possibly take their name from the 'bleus' of the Vendée who had fought the 'blancs', defenders of the Cross and the Crown. As Jean Gillet points out in his groundbreaking study, the over-sanctimonious God figure who requests compliments, praise and flattery may caricature some of the aspects of Napoleon, the head of France who had shown hubris in removing the imperial crown from the Pope's hands in order to set it on his own head. The Emperor who was a product of the Enlightenment seemed to be fast forgetting his own origins. Like God the Father who was revolted by Adam and Eve's behaviour 'chez moi, dans mes jardins', he showed no tolerance for libertines, free-thinkers or public opinion. Parny had embraced the cause of the Revolution when it broke out. He had attempted to take part in the creation of a new State. He had condemned the excesses of Catholicism. He was certainly, like his friends the *idéologues*, reluctant to back the transition from the Directoire to the Consulate and then to a fully-blown imperial regime. In a sense, Napoleon appeared to be turning his back on those to whom he owed his place. Ironically, a copy of the first edition of *Le Portefeuille volé*, with a binding bearing the imperial arms, now belongs to the Bibliothèque Nationale in Paris.

Parny certainly intended to counter the flourishing trade in pro-Christian literature of which *Le Génie du Christianisme* – written, as Chateaubriand himself indicates in a letter to Amable de Baudus, first and foremost as an answer to *La Guerre des Dieux* – is but one indication. He used the arms of the apologists in order to fight his own corner. In the same spirit as Voltaire in numerous articles of the *Dictionnaire philosophique*, he was attempting to show that the Bible was a collection of tales, like those recounted in other mythological traditions. *La Guerre des Dieux* had introduced a notion of relativity by showing that all religions were much of a muchness. In *Le Paradis perdu*, as in the earlier poem, Parny must be saluted for managing to include serious ideas in humorous texts while such authors as Chateaubriand or La Harpe were busy penning unreadable treatises on the question.

There are far fewer reactions to the *Paradis perdu*, or, indeed, the whole of *Le Portefeuille volé*, than to the *Guerre des Dieux*. This is probably in part because Parny's name was not on the title-page. Reviewers would not all have paid close attention to an anonymous collection of politically incorrect poems. Labouïsse, whose own verse was always a pale shadow of the *Poésies érotiques*, claims he reprimanded Parny for the book: 'Je suis bien fâché qu'il ait livré sa muse et son imagination à de pareils *tableaux*. Ses vers sont impies et cyniques; et certes, je le lui ai dit avec franchise, ce n'est pas dans un siècle de licence et d'immoralité qu'il devait se laisser *voler* un pareil *portefeuille*.'[111] Ever faithful, *La Revue philosophique et littéraire*, the *Décade*'s successor, encouraged readers to purchase the collection by publishing some of the *Déguisements de Vénus* and claiming that, though the author was not named, 'tous les lecteurs le devinent dès le premier vers...'[112]

Joubert's extreme judgement of Parny, dated 25 April 1807, was certainly based on texts like *Le Paradis perdu* and *Les Galanteries de la Bible* as well as *La Guerre des Dieux*:

> Des blasphèmes mielleux et des ordures vernissées (ou, le blasphème coule de sa plume avec douceur, comme un miel empoisonné). Il a mis les vases sacrés dans les latrines, et parfumé avec l'encens les ordures des mauvais lieux. Enfin, il a souillé le Ciel, sali les temples et mis sur les autels de la porcelaine et du musc. Il a le cœur et l'âme eunuques. Il ne se montre insinuant que parce qu'il est énervé. Son impuissance a quelque grâce.[113]

Le Paradis perdu was received with less uproar than the *Guerre des Dieux*: although condemned in Coutances during the *Restauration*,[114] it was never included on the Catholic Church's list of banned books, the *Index Librorum Prohibitorum*, unlike the earlier work, which would tend to indicate that it was all right to write poems which flirted with impiety as long as they did not enjoy huge commercial success. However Parny's text, of which this is the first separate edition, deserves to take its place in any history of Milton's fortune in France and of the mock-epic tradition.

Principles of this edition

The 1808 edition of Parny's complete works (*Œuvres complètes*, Paris, Debray, 1808, 5 vol.) serves as base text for this edition.

Spelling has been modernized throughout (e.g. temps rather than tems, tourments rather than tourmens, enfants and not enfans, éléments and not élémens, roulements and not roulemens, mouvements and not mouvemens, abîmes and not abymes, partout not par-tout, groupes not grouppes, tout à coup, not tout-à-coup, longtemps not long-tems, pôle not pole, différents not différens, printemps not printems, âme not ame, entrouvre not entr'ouvre, enchâssée not enchassée, amants not amans, galants not galans, allégresse and not alégresse, rouvre not r'ouvre, chute not chûte, déjà not déja, savants not savans). Accents have been systematically placed on capital letters.

Plurals of present participles (dévorans, brûlans, sanglans, bruyans, pleuvans, charmans, pesans, fleurissans etc.) have been kept with their spelling updated (i. e. dévorants and not dévorans).

Other amendments to the base text are described in the notes.

We would like to thank Susan Seth for her invaluable assistance in preparing the text.

Notes

[1] The inventory after her death was drawn up on 26 May 1758. See Marie-Claire Buxtorf, 'L'inventaire après décès de Geneviève de La Nux, mère de Jean-Baptiste et d'Évariste Parny' in *Archives de Bourbon*, Saint-Denis, December 1986, pp. 37-40.

[2] Pierre-Louis Ginguené, 'Épître à M. de Parny, qui m'avait donné un exemplaire de ses œuvres', *Almanach des Muses*, 1791, pp. 217-20.

[3] Pierre-Louis Ginguené (1748-1816) was a writer, musicologist and journalist. He was an essential cultural intermediary between France and Italy. He held important administrative functions under the revolutionary and imperial regimes. See Catriona Seth, 'Ginguené et Parny' in *Ginguené (1748 - 1816), idéologue et médiateur*, ed. by Édouard Guitton (Rennes: P.U.R., 1995), pp. 97-103.

[4] Letter to Rosette Pinczon du Sel, 14 August 1783 (Archives Pinczon du Sel). For a discussion of the correspondence between the former head of the Collège de Rennes and Auguste Pinczon du Sel's sister, see Catriona Seth, 'Parny revisité: les lettres de l'abbé du Chatellier à Rosette Pinczon du Sel', *Cahiers Roucher - André Chénier*, 16 (1997), 105-16.

[5] Letter to Rosette Pinczon du Sel, 30 August 1782 (Archives Pinczon du Sel).

[6] 'Je voulais faire un ecclésiastique de P. et l'envoyer en Sorbonne parce que j'étais assuré qu'il s'y fût distingué au-dessus de quiconque et qu'il eût été évêque. Le bourreau fut d'abord de mon avis, mais rendu à Paris, il me souffla dans la manche'. Letter to Rosette Pinczon du Sel, 29 February 1783 (Archives Pinczon du Sel).

[7] The original belongs to his half-brother's descendants. See Catriona Seth, *Évariste Parny (1753-1814)*, thèse, Université de Paris-Sorbonne (Paris IV), 1995, sous la direction de Sylvain Menant, p. 572. Tissot's presentation in the 1827 edition of Parny's *Poésies inédites* uses many of the same terms but gives further details.

[8] Archives Nationales (Paris), MM 494 *Séminaire Saint Firmin - Livre des pensionnaires depuis 1732*.

[9] See Raphaël Barquissau, *Les Poètes créoles du XVIIIe siècle* (Paris: Jean Vigneau, 1949).

[10] The Forges de Châteaubrun and the La Nux (or Lanux) families were related by marriage.

[11] See Parny's letter of 6 April 1787 to Geneviève Panon du Portail, Archives Départementales de la Réunion (Sainte-Clotilde) and Parny, *Lettres familières*, ed. by Raphaël Barquissau (Paris: Colin, 1929), pp. 8-9. There was a prepublication

of the Barquissau edition of Parny's letters in the *Revue d'Histoire Littéraire de la France* (hereafter *RHLF*) in 1928.

[12] Valère was the daughter of Léda, one of Paul Parny's Malagasy slaves. She was born on 9 May 1775. Her godmother was one of Parny's nieces, Marie-Anne-Geneviève Dolnay de Palmaroux. The poet's sister, Geneviève Panon du Portail, watched over the girl during her childhood. The will he drew up on 12 April 1761 included provision for a dowry of 5,000 livres left to Valère. The girl married in 1789, the year she turned 14. She is said to have been the grandmother of Célimène, a nineteenth-century singer and songwriter known as 'la Muse de la Saline'. According to Léon de Forges de Parny, Parny could have fathered more illegitimate children with slave girls. See his article, 'Évariste de Parny fut-il le père de plusieurs enfants naturels à l'Île Bourbon ?' in *Académie de l'Île de la Réunion – Bulletin*, 27 mai 1984, pp. 139–45.

[13] See Jacques Lemaire, 'Parny et la franc-maçonnerie', in *Études sur le dix-huitième siècle*, 2 (1975), 43–57, and his edition of *La Guerre des Dieux anciens et modernes* (Paris: Champion, 2002).

[14] The volumes were published at the end of the year in order to be presented as New Year's gifts. The one published at the end of 1776 bears the indication *Almanach des Muses 1777*, and so on.

[15] As a whole, the reviews in the press were favourable (see e.g. the *Année littéraire*).

[16] See François-René de Chateaubriand, *Mémoires d'Outre-Tombe*, ed. by Maurice Regard, Bibliothèque de la Pléiade (Paris: Gallimard, 1951), i. 139.

[17] Pierre-Louis Ginguené, 'Épître à M. de Parny, qui m'avait donné un exemplaire de ses œuvres', *Almanach des Muses*, 1791, pp. 217–20.

[18] Letter to Geneviève Panon du Portail, 28 August 1786, ADR Sainte-Clotilde and *RHLF*, 35 (1928), p. 411.

[19] He was often referred to as the 'chevalier de Parny'.

[20] Quoted in the *Isographie des hommes célèbres* (Paris: Mesnier, 1828–30), II. 152.

[21] Archives Nationales (Paris) MC Étude LXXXVI, 13 September 1787.

[22] Letter to Geneviève Panon du Portail, ADR and *RHLF*, 35 (1928), p. 428.

[23] Pinczon du Sel died in Cayenne in 1789, Bertin in Charleston in 1790.

[24] Chateaubriand, *Mémoires d'Outre-Tombe*, i. 139.

[25] The location of the letter is unknown. Extracts are quoted in various autograph catalogues. See the *Fichier Charavay* in the Bibliothèque Nationale, Département des Manuscrits.

[26] Archives Nationales (hereafter AN) (Paris), MS AA 66(683).

[27] Bibliothèque Nationale de France (hereafter BNF) (Paris), MS NAF 9193, f°1.

[28] See Catriona Seth, 'Un opéra *politiquement correct* sous le Directoire: *L'Alceste* de l'an V (1797)', *Tragédies tardives*, ed. by Pierre Frantz and François Jacob (Paris: Champion, 2002), pp. 169-77.

[29] AN F17 1215.

[30] AN F17 1296.

[31] AN AA 66(683). Parny accepted on 15 Vendémiaire an VII and sent his text on the 22nd of the same month.

[32] Constant Pierre, *Les Hymnes et Chansons de la Révolution, Aperçu général et Catalogue avec Notices historiques, analytiques et bibliographiques* (Paris: Imprimerie Nationale, 1904), p. 146.

[33] Fernand Drujon, *Catalogue des ouvrages, écrits et dessins de toute nature, poursuivis, supprimés ou condamnés depuis le 21 octobre 1814 jusqu'au 31 juillet 1877* (Paris: Rouveyre, 1879), p. 185.

[34] Charles-Jean-Auguste-Maximilien de Colnet du Ravel, *Les Étrennes de l'Institut National ou Revue littéraire de l'an VII* (Paris: Les Marchands de Nouveautés, an VII), p. 25.

[35] Quoted in Charles-Augustin Sainte-Beuve, *Correspondance générale*, ed. by Jean Bonnerot, 19 vols (Paris: Stock, 1935-83), v (1947), p. 428, n. 1.

[36] Sainte-Beuve, 'Parny' (1844) in *Causeries du lundi* (Paris: Garnier, 1862), pp. 285-86.

[37] *Décade*, 30 pluviôse an VII, p. 342.

[38] Letter to Amable de Baudus, in Chateaubriand, *Correspondance générale*, ed. by Béatrix d'Andlau et al., 7 vols (Paris: Gallimard, 1977), I. 91.

[39] Quoted in the *Bulletin du Bibliophile*, 1866, 32e année, p. 421.

[40] BNF, MS NAF 1307.

[41] BNF, MS Fonds maçonnique 290, pièce 107: *Table des membres de la L. des Neuf Sœurs*, Archives du G. O., n°5126bis, an 1806.

[42] Doctor Gerald Suskind came to the conclusion, after analysing the texts in which Parny refers to his illness, that he was probably suffering from lymphatic oedema possibly due to schistosomiasis or phyllaria bancrofti. See appendix V of Catriona Seth, *Évariste Parny (1753-1814)*.

⁴³ Béranger's text was set to music by Wilhem. See *Le Souvenir des Ménestrels*, 1816, pp. 94–97.

⁴⁴ Charles Baudelaire, letter to Madame Alphonse Baudelaire, in *Correspondance*, ed. by Claude Pichois and Jean Ziegler, Bibliothèque de la Pléiade, 2 vols (Paris: Gallimard, 1973), I. 134–35.

⁴⁵ Marcel Proust, *Le Côté de Guermantes* (1921), ed. by Jean-Yves Tadié, Bibliothèque de la Pléiade (Paris: Gallimard, 1988), II. 742–43.

⁴⁶ See Glynn Barratt, 'Eighteenth-century Neoclassical French Influences on E.A. Baratynsky and Pushkin', *Comparative Literature Studies*, 6 (1969), 435–461.

⁴⁷ Anna Akhmatova, *Poèmes* (Moscow: Radouga, 1992), p. 32.

⁴⁸ G.W.F. Hegel, *Aesthetics*, tr. by T.M. Knox (Oxford: Clarendon Press, 1975), p. 508.

⁴⁹ See Heinrich Heine, *Selected Prose*, tr. by Ritchie Robertson (London: Penguin, 1993), p. 276. Heine's debt to Parny was pointed out by Wolfgang Menzel, *Die deutsche Literatur*, 2nd, enlarged edn, 4 vols (Stuttgart: Hallberger'sche Verlagshandlung, 1836), IV. 338–39.

⁵⁰ R.-D. Keil, 'Parny-Anklänge im Evgenij Onegin', *Festschrift für Margarete Woltner zum 70. Geburtstag am 4. Dezember 1967*, ed. Peter Brang (Heidelberg: Winter, 1967), pp. 121–133.

⁵¹ Alexander Pushkin, *Eugene Onegin*, tr. by Charles Johnston (London: n. pub., 1977), p. 79 (presumably alluding to the *Poésies érotiques*). On the *Gavriliiad*, see John Bayley, *Pushkin: A Comparative Commentary* (Cambridge: Cambridge University Press, 1971), pp. 65–68.

⁵² Gustave Flaubert, *Madame Bovary*, ed. by Claudine Gothot-Mersch (Paris: Garnier, 1971), p. 93.

⁵³ Oskar Panizza, *Das Liebeskonzil und andere Schriften* (Neuwied: Luchterhand, 1964), pp. 146–49.

⁵⁴ Lucy Newlyn, *'Paradise Lost' and the Romantic Reader* (Oxford: Oxford University Press, 1993), p. x. Future citations in text.

⁵⁵ All quotations are from Milton, *Paradise Lost*, ed. by Alastair Fowler, 2nd edn revised (London: Pearson Education, 2007).

⁵⁶ A.J.A. Waldock, *Paradise Lost' and the Critics* (Cambridge: Cambridge University Press, 1947), p. 46.

⁵⁷ C.S. Lewis, *A Preface to 'Paradise Lost'* (London: Oxford University Press, 1942), p. 122. Cf. Nietzsche's polemical account in *On the Genealogy of Morals* (1887) of

how pagan heroic virtues were reinterpreted from a slave's viewpoint as vices, and slavish qualities revalued as Christian virtues.

[58] Stanley Eugene Fish, *Surprised by Sin: The Reader in Paradise Lost* (London: Macmillan, 1967).

[59] See Georges Ascoli, *La Grande-Bretagne devant l'opinion française au XVIIe siècle*, 2 vols (Paris: Librairie Universitaire J. Gamber, 1930), ii. 121-22.

[60] Studies of these translations are included in Jean Gillet's encyclopedic *Le Paradis perdu dans la littérature française: De Voltaire à Chateaubriand* (Paris: Klincksieck, 1975). Future citations in text.

[61] See Milton, *Christian Doctrine*, tr. by John Carey, in *Complete Prose Works of John Milton*, 8 vols (New Haven and London: Yale University Press, 1953-82), vi. 206-09. The question occupies the whole of Book I, chapter 5 (pp. 203-80).

[62] See John P. Rumrich, 'Milton's Arianism: Why it Matters', in *Milton and Heresy*, ed. by Stephen P. Dobranski and John P. Rumrich (Cambridge: Cambridge University Press, 1998), pp. 75-92 (p. 76).

[63] *Les Œuvres complètes de Voltaire / The Complete Works of Voltaire*, 135 vols (Geneva: Institut et Musée Voltaire; Oxford: Voltaire Foundation, 1968-), vol. iiiB: *The English essays of 1727*, ed. by David Williams (1996), p. 374. Future references to this edition are by volume and page number in the text. Voltaire's *Essay on Epick Poetry* was published in London in 1727; a French version, differing considerably, appeared in 1733.

[64] David Williams, 'Voltaire: literary critic', *SVEC* 48 (1966), 1-381 (p. 228); iiiB:206.

[65] Torquato Tasso, *Discourses on the Heroic Poem*, tr. by Mariella Cavalchini and Irene Samuel (Oxford: Clarendon Press, 1973), p. 38.

[66] *PL* i. 738-46; many French examples in R.A. Sayce, *The French Biblical Epic in the Seventeenth Century* (Oxford: Clarendon Press, 1955), pp. 166-68.

[67] Nicolas Boileau-Despréaux, *Épîtres, Art Poétique, Le Lutrin*, ed. by Charles-H. Boudhors (Paris: Société Les Belles Lettres, 1952), p. 102.

[68] *Encyclopédie ou Dictionnaire raisonné des sciences, des arts et des métiers*, ed. by Diderot and others, 17 vols (Paris: Briasson, etc., 1751-85), x. 393.

[69] William Empson, *Milton's God* (London: Chatto & Windus, 1961), p. 124.

[70] Alexander Pope, 'The First Epistle of the Second Book of *Horace*', lines 99-102, in *The Twickenham Edition of the Poems of Alexander Pope*, ed. by John Butt, 11 vols (London: Methuen and New Haven: Yale University Press, 1939-69), iv: Imitations of Horace, ed. by John Butt (1939), p. 203.

[71] Quoted in Empson, *Milton's God*, pp. 115–16.

[72] Pierre Bayle, *Dictionnaire historique et critique*, 4 vols (Amsterdam: Brunel, etc., 1730), III. 627 (article 'Pauliciens', note E).

[73] On God's character defects, see John Peter, *A Critique of 'Paradise Lost'* (London: Longmans, 1960); Neil Forsyth, *The Satanic Epic* (Princeton: Princeton University Press, 2003).

[74] This grimly humorous God is based on Psalm 2:4: 'He that sitteth in the heavens shall laugh; the Lord shall have them in derision.' For the possible influence of *Paradise Lost* on the (better-natured) humorous God of Goethe's *Faust I*, see Karl S. Guthke, 'Goethe, Milton und der humoristische Gott. Eine Studie zur poetischen Weltordnung im *Faust*', *Goethe*, 22 (1960), 104-11.

[75] Empson, *Milton's God*, p. 111.

[76] David Hume, *The Natural History of Religion*, ed. A. Wayne Colver, and *Dialogues Concerning Natural Religion*, ed. John Valdimir Price (Oxford: Clarendon Press, 1976), p. 82.

[77] Ibid., p. 83.

[78] 'Poème sur le désastre de Lisbonne' (1756), in *Œuvres complètes de Voltaire,* ed. by Louis Moland, 50 vols (Paris: Garnier, 1877–83), ix. 474. Henceforth cited as Moland with volume and page number in the text.

[79] [Nicolas-Antoine Boulanger], *Le Christianisme dévoilé, ou Examen des principes et des effets de la religion chrétienne* (London: n.pub., 1767), p. 87. The suggestion that Parny may have read Boulanger is made by J.-M. Apostolidès, 'Quand les dieux font la guerre', *Liberté*, 27 (October 1965), 111–20 (p. 114).

[80] See Stella Purce Revard, *The War in Heaven: 'Paradise Lost' and the Tradition of Satan's Rebellion* (Ithaca and London: Cornell University Press, 1980), p. 134.

[81] Samuel Johnson, *The Lives of the most Eminent English Poets; with Critical Observations on their Works*, ed. by Roger Lonsdale, 4 vols (Oxford: Clarendon Press, 2006), i. 290–91.

[82] Similar criticisms can be found among Milton's German readers: see Johann Christoph Gottsched, *Ausgewählte Werke*, ed. by Joachim Birke and Brigitte Birke, 12 vols (Berlin and New York: de Gruyter, 1968–95), vi/1. 238; August Wilhelm Schlegel, *Vorlesungen über Ästhetik I [1798–1803]*, ed. by Ernst Behler (Paderborn: Schöningh, 1989), pp. 630–34. Cf. also the well-known diatribe against Milton which Voltaire puts into the mouth of Pococurante in *Candide*, Moland xxi. 204. The world-weary Pococurante, however, is not to be taken as simply a mouthpiece for Voltaire's opinions.

[83] Jean-François Marmontel, 'Essai sur le goût', in his *Éléménts de littérature*, ed. by Sophie Le Ménahèze (Paris: Desjonquères, 2005), p. 46. See also the articles

'Description', 'Éloquence poétique', 'Enthousiasme', 'Épopée', 'Fiction' and 'Merveilleux'. All except the last, which deplores the puerile and absurd danger faced by the angels and their fight against the devils, are full of praise for the English poem.

[84] *The Spectator*, no. 297, Saturday, February 9, 1712, in Joseph Addison and others, *The Spectator*, ed. by Donald Bond, 5 vols (Oxford: Clarendon Press, 1965), iii. 60. Addison qualifies his judgement, however, in *The Spectator*, no. 309, Saturday, February 23, 1712 (ib., iii. 119).

[85] See T.S. Eliot, 'Milton II', in his *On Poetry and Poets* (London: Faber, 1957), pp. 146-61 (p. 156).

[86] *Lettres critiques sur le Paradis perdu et reconquis de Milton* (Paris, 1731), quoted in Gillet, p. 143.

[87] Constantin de Magny, *Dissertation critique sur le Paradis perdu, poème héroïque de Milton* (Paris, 1731), quoted in Gillet, p. 143.

[88] Quoted in Gillet, p. 216. The real beauty of this passage is illuminated by Empson's remark that as it is evening, the angel can slide 'down a nearly *even* sunbeam, like the White Knight on the poker': see William Empson, 'Milton and Bentley', in *Some Versions of Pastoral* (London: Chatto & Windus, 1935), pp. 147-91 (pp. 157-58).

[89] *The Spectator*, no. 297 (iii. 59).

[90] 'Dedication of the *Æneis*' (1697), in *Essays of John Dryden*, ed. by W.P. Ker, 2 vols (Oxford: Clarendon Press, 1926), ii. 165. Cf. John Dennis: 'the Devil is properly his Hero, because he gets the better' – 'The Grounds of Criticism in Poetry' (1704) in *The Critical Works of John Dennis*, ed. by Edward Niles Hooker, 2 vols (Baltimore: The Johns Hopkins Press, 1943), i. 334.

[91] Marmontel, 'Enthousiasme', p. 485.

[92] Letter to William Nicol, 18 June 1787, in *The Letters of Robert Burns*, ed. by G. Ross Roy, 2 vols (Oxford: Clarendon Press, 1985), i. 123.

[93] 'The Marriage of Heaven and Hell', in *Blake: Complete Writings*, ed. by Geoffrey Keynes (London: Oxford University Press, 1957), p. 150.

[94] Bayle, *Dictionnaire*, iii. 393.

[95] A slight misquotation from *PL* 383-84: 'Among unequals what society | Can sort, what harmony or true delight?' The same misquotation occurs in a letter of 21 December 1741 from Voltaire to Frederick the Great (D2573 in *Correspondence and related documents*, ed. by Theodore Besterman, 51 vols (Geneva: Institut et Musée Voltaire, 1970-77), viii (1970), p. 151).

⁹⁶ Friedrich Schiller, *Sämtliche Werke*, ed. Gerhard Fricke and Herbert G. Göpfert, 5 vols (Munich: Hanser, 1958), i. 918. This passage did not appear in the published version of the play.

⁹⁷ Percy Bysshe Shelley, 'A Defence of Poetry', in *The Complete Works of Percy Bysshe Shelley*, ed. by Roger Ingpen and Walter E. Peck, 10 vols (London: Benn, 1926-30), vii. 109-40 (p. 129). Cf. Shelley's more critical account of Satan in the Preface to *Prometheus Unbound*, discussed by Newlyn, pp. 146-47.

⁹⁸ Xavier de Maistre, *Voyage autour de ma chambre*, ed. by Florence Lotterie (Paris: GF Flammarion, 2003), pp. 115-16.

⁹⁹ For various views on the political interpretation of Satan's rebellion, see Christopher Hill, *Milton and the English Revolution* (London: Faber, 1977); Blair Worden, 'Milton's republicanism and the tyranny of heaven', in *Machiavelli and Republicanism*, ed. by Gisela Bock, Quentin Skinner and Maurizio Viroli (Cambridge: Cambridge University Press, 1990), pp. 225-45; Newlyn, pp. 91-97; David Norbrook, *Writing the English Republic: Poetry, Rhetoric and Politics, 1627-1660* (Cambridge: Cambridge University Press, 1999), pp. 433-95; Worden, *Literature and Politics in Cromwellian England* (Oxford: Oxford University Press, 2007).

¹⁰⁰ See Mario Praz, *The Romantic Agony*, tr. by Angus Davidson, 2nd edn (London: Oxford University Press, 1970), ch. 2: 'The Metamorphoses of Satan'.

¹⁰¹ *Le Pére Goriot*, in Honoré de Balzac, *La Comédie humaine*, ed. by Pierre-Georges Castex, Bibliothèque de la Pléiade, 12 vols (Paris: Gallimard, 1976-81), iii. 219.

¹⁰² *Encyclopédie*, iii. 158.

¹⁰³ Milton, *Christian Doctrine*, vi. 351-52.

¹⁰⁴ Ibid., pp. 383-84.

¹⁰⁵ See Jonathan Israel, *Radical Enlightenment: Philosophy and the Making of Modernity 1650-1750* (Oxford: Oxford University Press, 2001), pp. 87-88.

¹⁰⁶ St Augustine, *Concerning the City of God against the Pagans*, tr. by Henry Bettenson (London: Penguin, 1984), p. 567 (xiv. 10).

¹⁰⁷ Ibid., p. 591 (xiv. 26).

¹⁰⁸ See William Poole, *Milton and the Idea of the Fall* (Cambridge: Cambridge University Press, 2005), esp. pp. 22-30.

¹⁰⁹ Torquato Tasso, *Gerusalemme Liberata*, ed. by Bruno Maier, Biblioteca Universale Rizzoli (Milan: Rizzoli, 1982), p. 565 (xvi. 15).

[110] *Godfrey of Bulloigne: A critical edition of Edward Fairfax's translation of Tasso's 'Gerusalemme Liberata', together with Fairfax's Original Poems*, ed. by Kathleen M. Lea and T.M. Gang (Oxford: Clarendon Press, 1981), p. 452.

[111] Auguste de Labouïsse, *Souvenirs et Mélanges* (Paris: Bossange, 1826), p. 271.

[112] *La Revue philosophique et littéraire*, an XIII, 1er trimestre, pp. 241–43.

[113] Joseph Joubert, *Pensées, jugements et notations* (Paris: José Corti, 1989), pp. 289–90.

[114] 'Destruction ordonnée par jugement du Tribunal correctionnel de Coutances, du 30 août 1826' in Fernand Drujon, *Catalogue des ouvrages, écrits et dessins de toute nature, poursuivis, supprimés ou condamnés depuis le 21 octobre 1814 jusqu'au 31 juillet 1877* (Paris: Rouveyre, 1879), p. 297.

LE PARADIS PERDU

LE PARADIS PERDU,
POÈME.

~~~~~~~~~~~

CHANT PREMIER.

Je suis dévot, et le serai toujours.[1]
Brûlez ces vers où mon jeune délire
A soupiré de profanes amours.[2]
Je dois, hélas! expier mes beaux jours.
Aux chants chrétiens j'ai donc voué ma lyre.
Vous, qui l'aimiez, par le temps avertis,
Ainsi que moi, vous êtes convertis,
Et j'obtiendrai votre pieux sourire.
Le Saint-Esprit veut qu'en vers ingénus
Je vous raconte Éden, le premier homme,
La jolie Ève, et le diable et la pomme.
Doit-on chanter les biens qu'on a perdus?

    L'ange rebelle et sa nombreuse armée,
Depuis neuf mois[3] par le foudre rival
Précipités dans le gouffre infernal,
Nus sur les flots d'une mer enflammée,
Roulaient encor, faibles, muets d'horreur,[4]
Sans mouvement, et non pas sans douleur.

---

[1] The opening passage of *La Guerre des Dieux* also shows the narrator claiming to be 'dévot'.

[2] Initial allusive reference to Parny's *Poésies érotiques* (1778). See also note 39 below.

[3] Transformed from the nine days and nights that it takes Milton's rebel angels to fall from heaven to hell (PL i. 50).

[4] We have corrected 'horreurs' on the basis of the rhyme scheme and of earlier editions.

Satan enfin par degrés se ranime,
Ouvre les yeux, contemple sans effroi
L'affreux séjour où le plongea son crime,
Parle et sa voix emplit le vaste abîme:
« Horrible enfer, obéis à ton roi. »
Il a repris sa force et son courage;
Trois fois du lac ses ailes et sa main
Frappent les feux; il s'élève soudain,
Vole et descend sur le brûlant rivage.
« Tourments nouveaux et pires que la mort,
Dit-il, cessez. » Espérance trop vaine!
Ses pieds tremblaient; il rend avec effort
L'air enflammé qu'il aspire avec peine.
Il reconnaît sur les flots dévorants
Ses compagnons étendus, expirants;
De son destin il voit l'horreur entière,
Des pleurs cruels humectent sa paupière,
Et de son cœur, qui se trouble un moment,
S'échappe un long et sourd gémissement.
Mais tout à coup rappelant son audace,
D'une voix forte il crie: « Esprits[5] divins,
Principautés, Archanges, Séraphins,
Enfants du ciel, est-ce là votre place?
Pour vous ce lit aurait-il des attraits?
Debout, debout tout à l'heure, ou jamais. »
Il parle encor; cette voix redoutée,
Par cent échos à la fois répétée,
Termine enfin leur douloureux sommeil.
Un long murmure annonce leur réveil.
Leur vol ressemble au bruit sourd de l'orage
Roulant au loin de nuage en nuage.
Du lac brûlant ils atteignent les bords,
Et sans frayeur, sans plaintes, sans remords,
Ils s'arment tous: leurs mains impatientes
Livrent aux vents les enseignes brillantes.
Satan, pareil à la cime d'un mont
Où l'ouragan tonne et rugit sans cesse,
Au milieu d'eux lève son noble front

---

[5] The final s of the plural has been included on the basis of earlier editions.

Qu'a sillonné la foudre vengeresse;⁶
Et dit: « Amis, qu'en cet affreux séjour
L'unité triple exile sans retour,
Nous méritions un plus heureux partage.
Tout ce que peut l'ennui de l'esclavage,
Un juste orgueil par l'orgueil accablé,
La valeur calme, et l'audace et la rage,
Nous l'avons fait: les tyrans ont tremblé;
Ils pâlissaient sur leur trône ébranlé:
La foudre seule a vaincu le courage.
Mais aux vaincus il reste la fierté,
L'horreur du joug, le cri de liberté,
La haine enfin consolante et cruelle,
La haine active, implacable, éternelle.
Si toutefois à des dangers nouveaux
Vous préférez la honte du repos,
Parlez sans crainte; ici l'on peut tout dire;
À d'autres mains je remettrai l'empire,
Et j'irai seul, sans espoir et sans peur,
Dans son triomphe attaquer le vainqueur. »
   Le sage Ammos⁷ pour répondre s'avance:
« Illustre chef, généraux et soldats,
Du triple Dieu vous savez la puissance.
Pourquoi sur nous aggraver sa vengeance?
Nous payons cher l'orgueil de nos combats.
Loin d'irriter sa foudre à peine éteinte,
Aimons la nuit qui nous cache à ses yeux.
L'adresse et l'art peuvent changer ces lieux.
Que trouvons-nous dans cette horrible enceinte?
Un air infect et lourd, des rocs brûlants,
Des mers de feu, des gouffres, des volcans.
De tous ces corps vous extrairez sans peine

---

⁶ Cf. PL i. 600–01: 'but his face | Deep scars of thunder had intrenched'.

⁷ In the Bible, Moloch is the divinity of the Ammonites. Parny's character of Ammos the chemist may owe his existence to Antoine-Laurent de Lavoisier, the father of modern chemistry, executed on 8 May 1794 after the judge had famously remarked that the Republic had no need for scientists. His contribution to the infernal debate corresponds to that of Milton's Belial, who argues that hell may in time become bearable.

Carbone, azote,[8] oxygène,[9] hydrogène,[10]
Et calorique[11] (il abonde aux enfers);
Recomposez ces éléments divers,
Variez-les; sous votre main féconde
De nouveaux corps naîtront subitement.
Pour être dieux ici, pour faire un monde,
Vous avez tout, matière et mouvement. »
 Le dur Moloch lève sa tête altière,
Et d'une voix qui ressemble au tonnerre:
« À toi permis, Ammos, d'analyser
Ces feux ardents, de les recomposer.
Refais l'enfer; ce travail est utile.
Mais veux-tu donc en chimiste tranquille
Changer Moloch? Autour de tes fourneaux
Retiendras-tu ce peuple de héros?
Non, certes, non. Si ta chimie est bonne,
Elle aurait dû fondre le fer maudit
Qui dans le ciel deux fois te pourfendit.
Je connais peu l'azote et le carbone;
Je sais la guerre, et la ferai; j'ai dit. »
 Moloch se tait; l'infernal auditoire
De sa harangue approuve la vigueur,
Et dans les rangs circule un bruit flatteur.
De la chimie Ammos défend la gloire;
Satan se lève, et du fourreau brillant
Tirant soudain son glaive étincelant:
D'un bras nerveux sur sa tête il l'agite.
L'armée entière avec transport l'imite;
Un million de glaives et d'éclairs

---

[8] Nitrogen was discovered in 1772 by Daniel Rutherford. Its French name, chosen by Antoine-Laurent de Lavoisier, indicates that it is 'without life' since, unlike oxygen, it does not maintain animal life. Like oxygen and hydrogen, it was a newly isolated element. None of the four words, *Carbone*, *Azote*, *Oxygène* or *Hydrogène* figures in the An VII (1799) edition of the *Dictionnaire de l'Académie française*.

[9] Oxygen was a recent discovery by the Swedish scientist Carl Wilhelm Scheele in 1771. His research was not widely known and the element was identified independently by Joseph Priestley and named, in 1774, by Lavoisier.

[10] Henry Cavendish discovered *inflammable* air in 1766, and Lavoisier named it hydrogen.

[11] Lavoisier, amongst others, thought that heat was a material substance.

Jettent dans l'ombre une clarté subite;
Les étendards s'élèvent dans les airs;
Le fifre aigu, le trombone barbare,
Et des tambours les roulements divers,
Et du combat la bruyante fanfare,
Portent au ciel le défi des enfers.
   Satan alors: « Vous, qu'on nomme rebelles,
Vous, à l'honneur, à la raison fidèles,
De l'esclavage éternels ennemis,
Pour la vengeance à jamais réunis,
À la valeur alliez la prudence.
Ne livrons point des combats incertains.
De l'oppresseur épions en silence
Les mouvements, le repos, les desseins.
Il peut créer, mais nous pouvons détruire;
Entre nous donc se partage l'empire.
Pour repeupler son triste paradis,
Je sais qu'il doit inventer d'autres êtres,
Moins grands, moins purs, d'un vil limon[12] pétris,
Propres enfin à ramper sous des maîtres.
Je sais de plus que ces êtres chéris
Habiteront une prison lointaine
Où quelque temps ils feront quarantaine:[13]
Au Ciel ensuite ils pourront être admis:
La Trinité traite mal ses amis.
Il faut les voir, connaître leur nature,
Leurs passions, leurs défauts, et leurs goûts.
Quel coup heureux d'attirer parmi nous
Nos successeurs! au tyran quelle injure!
Oui, mes amis, c'est dans la créature
Qu'il faut frapper, blesser le créateur.
Qu'en pensez vous? » Un long *bravo* s'élève,
Des antres noirs perce la profondeur,
Résonne au loin, décroît avec lenteur,
Décroît encore, et meurt. Satan achève:
« De ce projet le succès est douteux,

---

[12] 'Limon' is the standard term for the clay from which Adam is said to have been formed.

[13] Here Parny introduces the doctrine of Purgatory, absent from *Paradise Lost*.

Et les dangers sont certains et nombreux.
Il faut d'abord, sans clartés et sans guide,
D'un pied prudent ou d'une aile timide,
Sonder, franchir des abîmes nouveaux,
Des régions immenses et désertes,
D'autres encor de ruines couvertes,
Et traverser l'empire du chaos;
Il faut ouvrir les redoutables portes
Que du vainqueur la main scella sur nous;
Et là sans doute, inquiet et jaloux,
Il a placé de nombreuses cohortes.
Par quel miracle échapper à leurs yeux,
Au qui-va-là des vedettes prudents,
Aux promeneurs, aux patrouilles errantes
Qui jour et nuit se croisent dans les cieux?
Ce projet donc exige un esprit sage,
La fermeté, l'adresse, le courage;
Et son succès change notre avenir.
Qui d'entre vous osera l'accomplir? »
Chacun se tait; après un long silence,[14]
Satan reprend: « Le premier en puissance
Dans les dangers doit le premier courir.
Demeurez donc, et seul je vais partir. »
D'autres *bravo*, bien mérités sans doute,
Du vaste enfer ébranlèrent la voûte.

    On se sépare; et chacun du repos
Diversement abrège la durée.
L'ennui partout est le pire des maux.
L'un prend sa lyre ou sa harpe dorée,
Et dans un hymne en silence écouté,
Sa noble voix chante la liberté.
L'autre plus gai, sur les airs des cantiques,
Psalmodiant des couplets satiriques,
Livre aux sifflets l'auguste Trinité.[15]
Sur un coteau sans fleurs et sans verdure
D'où jaillissaient des tourbillons de feux,

---

[14] We have corrected a semi-colon by inserting a comma in its place.
[15] Perhaps an allusion to the fact that many revolutionary songs were set to the tunes of hymns.

Mille démons, en cinq actes pompeux,
Représentaient leur tragique aventure.
Oui, dans l'enfer naquit cet art charmant,
De l'homme instruit noble délassement.
De promeneurs on voit partout des groupes.
D'autres dansaient en rond. D'autres par troupes
Cherchent au loin quelque monde meilleur;
Des monts fumants ils gravissent les cimes,
Brisent les rocs et comblent les abîmes,
Et des enfers sondent la profondeur.
Ammos fait mieux: dans ses calculs tranquilles
Il cherche, il trouve un monde régulier;
Puis, s'entourant d'opérateurs habiles,
Dans le creuset il met l'enfer entier.
    Loin d'eux Satan poursuivait son voyage
Plus périlleux que les sanglants combats,
Et sans secours, seul avec son courage,
Dans le chaos il égarait ses pas.
D'objets divers un informe assemblage
À ses regards s'offre confusément.
Sur son chemin naissent subitement
Le chaud, le froid, et le sec et l'humide,
La flamme et l'onde, et le plein et le vide.
Contre un obstacle il heurte à tout moment.
Il tombe, il monte, il recule, il avance.
À son oreille éclate quelquefois
Un bruit soudain que suit un prompt silence;
Mais parle-t-il? tout est sourd et sans voix.
Il monte encore, et des ombres nouvelles,
De nouveaux chocs le retardent en vain:
Des mains, des pieds, de la tête et des ailes,
Avec effort il se fraye un chemin.
Il traversait les flammes dévorantes,
Les tourbillons et les trombes errantes.
L'air tout à coup se dérobe sous lui,
Et vainement son bras cherche un appui;
Rapide il tombe, ainsi qu'un météore
Qui fend les airs, et tomberait encore,
Si le hasard dans ce lieu n'eût placé

De gaz divers un amas condensé.[16]
Frappant du pied l'élastique nuage,
Tel qu'un ballon l'archange rebondit,
S'élève, puis retombe, et s'engloutit
Dans un marais sans fond et sans rivage.
Autre hasard trop funeste; un volcan
Sous ce marais subitement s'allume,
Et dans les airs lance au loin le bitume,
Les rocs fondus, et la boue, et Satan.
L'éruption terrible, mais utile,
Lui fait franchir trois cents milles et plus.
Il trouve alors un chemin plus facile,
Traverse en paix des déserts inconnus,
Et voit enfin la centuple barrière
Qui doit des cieux protéger la frontière.
Il ne sait pas qu'aux sept péchés mortels
De Jéhova les ordres solennels
Ont confié cet important passage.
Pour le forcer, déjà brûlant de rage
Il s'avançait: la Colère et l'Orgueil,
Toujours armés et debout sur le seuil,
Jetant un cri, sur lui fondent ensemble.
Mais aussitôt reconnaissant ses traits,
À ses genoux ils tombent satisfaits.
La troupe entière à ses pieds se rassemble.
Seul autrefois il lui donna le jour.
Lorsqu'ennuyé de la céleste cour,
Morne et pensif sur sa fuite prochaine
Il méditait, sept fois sa forte main
D'un coup heureux frappa son front divin
Et de ce front jaillirent non sans peine
Les sept enfants qui, dociles et doux,
Dans ce moment embrassent ses genoux.[17]

---

[16] Parny's use of the word 'gaz', first recorded in French only in 1787, attests an interest in science which is very much in the spirit of Milton: cf. Satan's encountering 'The strong rebuff of some tumultuous cloud | Instinct with fire and nitre' (*PL* ii. 936-37).

[17] Allusion to the Greek myth according to which Athene was born from the head of Zeus, and adapted by Milton to make Sin spring from the head of Satan (*PL* ii. 753-58). The seven children here are the Christian deadly sins, as Wrath, Pride and Lust indicate.

Il les relève, et dit à la Luxure,
Qu'environnaient de lubriques beautés:
« D'où te vient donc cette progéniture?
Il n'est point d'anges en ces lieux écartés.
– Non, et pourtant je désire et je brûle;
Un feu vainqueur dans mes veines circule.
Avec ce doigt je presse doucement...
– Quoi donc? – Mon front; et chaque attouchement,
Chaque plaisir est suivi d'une fille.
– Augmente encore ta nombreuse famille.
Moi, je poursuis mon pénible dessein.
Allons, enfants, secondez votre père;
Ouvrons, brisons ces cent portes d'airain;[18]
Et seul je vais recommencer la guerre. »
Il dit; bientôt sur leurs énormes gonds
Avec fracas les cent portes fatales
Roulent; ce bruit dans les gouffres profonds
Pénètre, passe aux rives infernales;
Et des démons le hurlement[19] joyeux
Soudain s'élève et menace les cieux.

FIN DU CHANT PREMIER

=================================

CHANT SECOND.

J'ai trop souffert dans les brûlants abîmes;
Assez longtemps j'y plongeai mes lecteurs,
Gens délicats, d'un air pur amateurs,
Et de mes vers innocentes victimes.

---

[18] Babylon, rather than Heaven, is usually said to have had a hundred bronze doors.
[19] We have corrected the plural on the basis of earlier editions and because the verb which follows is in the singular.

Après Milton, dans ces gouffres maudits
C'est à regret que ma muse est tombée.
Faisons, messieurs, une heureuse enjambée,
Et de l'enfer sautons en paradis.
    Un Chérubin, c'est-à-dire deux ailes,
De blonds cheveux, un visage joufflu,[20]
Fend comme un trait les plaines éternelles,
Arrive, et dit: «Seigneur, mes yeux ont vu
Sur la frontière un des anges rebelles,
Qui, de ses fers, par la ruse échappé,[21]
Marche sans bruit, dans l'ombre enveloppé. »
En souriant la Trinité l'écoute,
Et lui répond avec grâce et bonté:
« Je sais cela de toute éternité.
– Vous le saviez, Dieu prévoyant? – Sans doute.
– S'il est ainsi, messeigneurs,[22] de l'enfer
À quoi servaient les cents portes de fer?
– Fit-on jamais une prison sans porte?
– Mais on la ferme. – Aussi la fermait-on,
La gardait-on; bien ou mal, il n'importe.
– Désirez-vous votre gros foudre? – Non.
– Malheur à l'homme! – À la tentation
S'il cède, il meurt. – Ô sagesse! ô clémence!
Permettez-nous du moins de renverser
L'arbre fatal[23]. – Osez-vous y penser?
– C'est prévenir un grand malheur –. Silence!
Vous le savez, je suis le Dieu jaloux;[24]
Je n'aime pas les têtes qui raisonnent.
Qu'autour de moi les louanges résonnent.
Point d'examen, ou craignez mon courroux.[25] »
À peine il dit, et les neuf chœurs des anges,

---

[20] *La Guerre des Dieux*, in Canto II, already pokes fun at the iconographic representations of cherubim as blond-haired heads with two wings.

[21] We have corrected a typographic error (échappés).

[22] Plural, because addressed to the Trinity.

[23] In Christian iconography, trees are generally the symbol of the cross. Here, it is the tree bearing the fruit of knowledge in the garden of Eden which is directly referred to by Satan.

[24] A quotation from Exodus 20:5: 'I the Lord thy God am a jealous God'.

[25] We have changed a colon into a full stop.

Saisis de peur, lui braillent des louanges.
Le *Te Deum,* l'éternel *Hosanna,*
L'*In excelsis,* le triste *Alleluia,*[26]
Des Triumdieux[27] charment l'oreille dure,
Et de plaisir ils battent la mesure.
    Durant ces chants, du nouvel univers
Satan sans peine a franchi la limite,
Et ses regards dans les mondes divers
Cherchent longtemps le point que l'homme habite.
Il voit enfin l'archange radieux
Qui dirigeait l'astre de la lumière;
Car le soleil, qui semble roi des cieux,
Roulait alors autour de notre terre:
L'homme depuis, changeant l'ordre divin,
Au firmament l'a cloué de sa main,
Et c'est la terre à présent qui voyage.
L'adroit Satan compose son visage;
Il adoucit son maintien fier et dur,
Décroît d'un pied, et prend d'un ange obscur
Les traits, l'habit, la voix humble et timide.[28]
– « Noble Azaël,[29] dit-il, en s'inclinant,
Vous, du très-haut le digne confident,
Apprenez-moi dans quel astre réside
De notre Dieu le favori nouveau?
Du genre humain où donc est le berceau?»
Volant toujours, et sans tourner la vue,
Sans saluer cet obscur immortel,
Négligemment le seigneur Azaël
Montre du doigt un point dans l'étendue,
Et dit: « Mon cher, c'est là. » Faux et bénin,
L'autre s'incline, et poursuit son chemin,

---

[26] This whole passage in which God claims to like being praised, and all present are made to sing various sacred tunes, is reminiscent of Canto II of *La Guerre des Dieux*.

[27] Neologism based on *Triumvirat* which serves to ridicule the Trinity, at which Parny had already taken a swipe in *La Guerre des Dieux*.

[28] Cf. *PL* iii. 636, where Satan assumes the form of a 'stripling cherub'.

[29] The name may have been suggested by Milton's 'Azazel' (*PL* i. 534). In *Paradise Lost*, the archangel of the sun is Uriel.

En répétant: « De ce faquin[30] peut-être
Aurais-je dû rabaisser la hauteur;
Quel air capable et quel ton protecteur
Prend ce valet dans l'absence du maître! »
    Par un vent frais rapidement porté
Sur notre globe enfin Satan arrive.
Là rien n'échappe à sa vue attentive.
En contemplant ce chef-d'œuvre vanté,
Il souriait avec malignité.
« Pourquoi, dit-il, refuser la lumière
Au double pôle, à cette zone entière,
Et les livrer à d'éternels frimas?
L'ours pourra seul habiter ces climats.
Sous l'équateur l'ardente canicule,
Un océan de sable, et des déserts,
Font regretter la rigueur des hivers.
Grand Jéhova, ce globe est ridicule.
Quoi? Dans les champs destinés aux moissons
Bénignement tu sèmes des poisons?
Quoi? tu te plais à créer les vipères,
Les scorpions, les serpents, les panthères,
Tigres, vautours, et requins dévorants?
Quelle douceur! que tes bienfaits sont grands!
J'aime à te voir entasser les nuages,
Du sud au nord promener les orages,
Et renverser les innocents sapins,
Faute de mieux: bientôt sur les humains
Tu lanceras ta foudre paternelle.[31]
Je ne hais pas ces fleuves débordés,
De ces volcans l'invention nouvelle,
Ces champs féconds de laves inondés.
J'approuve aussi la grêle meurtrière,

---

[30] *Faquin* is a contemptuous term for a worthless individual.

[31] The charge of futile and unjust violence, here transferred to the Christian God, was levelled against Zeus in Lucian's dialogue 'Zeus Catechized': 'Why in the world is it that […] you repeatedly blast an oak or a stone or the mast of a harmless ship, and now and then an honest and pious wayfarer?' (*The Works of Lucian*, tr. by A.M. Harmon, 8 vols, Loeb Classical Library (London: Heinemann, 1929), ii. 81). Parny had already used the idea in Canto II of *La Guerre des Dieux*, where the Virgin Mary tries unsuccessfully to dissuade God from using his unfair powers to wreak havoc on humanity.

Les ouragans, les tremblements de terre,
Présents fâcheux, que ta sage rigueur
Destine au juste aussi bien qu'au pécheur. »
    Il voit Éden: trois remparts de verdure
Environnaient ce jardin enchanté.
Il les franchit avec légèreté.
De ces beaux lieux voulez-vous la peinture?
On y trouvait tout ce qu'on trouve ailleurs,
Des fleurs, des fruits, et des fruits, et des fleurs,
De verts gazons, des grottes, des bocages,
De mille oiseaux les différents ramages,
Tous les parfums, un printemps éternel,
Un air plus pur, une plus fraîche aurore,
De clairs ruisseaux, puis des ruisseaux encore
D'argent potable, et de crème et de miel.[32]
    De ce jardin Ève était la merveille.
Auprès d'Adam, à l'ombre d'un bosquet,
Négligemment elle forme un bouquet,
Le jette ensuite, et sa bouche vermeille
Laisse échapper un long soupir d'ennui:
« Qu'avec lenteur le temps coule aujourd'hui!
– Occupons-nous. – Volontiers; mais que faire?
– Cueillons des fleurs. – Toujours des fleurs! – Eh bien,
Chantons un hymne. – Oh! je ne chante rien.
– Dormons. – Encor? Dînons, pour nous distraire.
– Je n'ai pas faim. Un seul fruit me plairait.
Du bien, du mal, il donne la science.
On nous défend d'y toucher. – La défense
Est très formelle,[33] et Dieu nous punirait,
Si … – Je le sais. – Je crains ton imprudence.
– Mais sous nos yeux, dis-moi, pourquoi planter
L'arbre fatal? est-ce pour nous tenter?
– On le croirait. – Je hais mon ignorance.
– En la perdant tu perdras ton bonheur.
– Mon bonheur? – Oui. – J'aime autant le malheur. »
    Le bon Adam l'approuve dans son âme,

---

[32] A reminiscence of Milton's 'potable gold' (*PL* iii. 608), but transferred from the sun to Eden and an allusion to the biblical 'land flowing with milk and honey' (Joshua 5:6).

[33] We have corrected the masculine form *formel*.

Et hautement il la gronde et la blâme.
Satan près d'eux s'était glissé sans bruit,
Et dit tout bas: « On leur défend ce fruit!
Bon! Je les tiens; ma victoire est certaine;
De l'ignorance on triomphe sans peine.
Quoi? leur hymen et leur jeune beauté,
L'occasion[34] sans cesse renaissante,
Ces lits de fleurs, cette ombre bienfaisante,
Les bains communs, l'entière nudité,
N'éveillent point leurs sens? Quelle injustice!
Du Dieu jaloux quel étrange caprice!
Mais sans amour peut-on multiplier?
Sottise, erreur! j'y veux remédier. »
    À quelques pas alors il se retire,
Prend des élus le gracieux sourire,
Et s'entourant d'un cercle radieux,
Des deux époux il éblouit les yeux.
Adam s'incline et dit: « Esprit céleste,
Soyez béni; parlez, qu'ordonnez-vous? »
Ève se tait; mais sa rougeur modeste
Est pour l'archange un compliment plus doux.
Il leur répond: « De Dieu dernier ouvrage,
Heureux Adam, et vous, dont les attraits
Manquent au ciel, un sinistre message
M'a prévenu de vos dangers secrets.
Loin de ces lieux, loin et trop près encore,
On a cru voir l'un des anges déchus.

        ADAM.[35]

Serait-il vrai? Tous mes sens sont émus.
Que cherche-t-il dans les cieux?

---

[34] The term was frequently used in a libertine context to refer to an opportunity for seducing a woman.

[35] Parny often uses the dialogue form in his verse, most notably in canto VI of *La Guerre des Dieux* when a dead man arrives in heaven. In *Les Galanteries de la Bible*, originally published in the same volume as *Le Paradis perdu*, God, Adam and Eve discuss the Fall of Man in a rhyming dialogue.

SATAN.

>Je l'ignore;
Mais s'il vous voit, je tremblerai pour vous.

ÈVE.

Emploira[36]-t-il la force?

SATAN.

>Non, l'adresse.

ÈVE.

S'il est ainsi, je crains peu son courroux.

ADAM.

Ève, du moins craignons notre faiblesse.

ÈVE.

Mais pourquoi donc tant d'immortels esprits
Par le Seigneur ont-ils été proscrits?

SATAN.

À tout moment il répète à ses anges:
« Obéissez, et chantez mes louanges.[37] »
Le fier Satan que fatiguaient ces mots,
Et qu'enrouaient les éternels cantiques,
Osa former des projets schismatiques,
Et chaque jour des prétextes nouveaux
Le dispensaient du plain-chant monotone.
Dieu le cita deux fois devant son trône.
L'ange irrité s'écria: « Sous sa loi

---

[36] The verbal form has been kept for the purposes of versification.
[37] This is reminiscent of *La Guerre des Dieux*.

De ma raison dois-je abjurer l'usage?
Non, le néant plutôt que l'esclavage![38]
Toujours chanter, toujours louer! Ma foi,
Je n'y tiens pas: compagnons, je déserte,
Et vais chercher quelque étoile déserte.
Loin des tyrans et de leurs plats élus;
J'y serai libre, et ne chanterai plus. »
Il partit donc; des légions entières
L'applaudissaient et suivirent ses pas.
Il réunit leurs nombreuses bannières,
Et sans frayeur attendit les combats.
Ils furent longs, incertains, et terribles.
Le paradis deux fois sur ses remparts
Des révoltés a vu les étendards.
Comme leur chef ils semblaient invincibles.
La foudre enfin les a du haut des airs
Précipités jusqu'au fond des enfers.

ÈVE.

J'ai cru Satan plus coupable.

ADAM.

Ma chère,
Vous aimez peu le chant et la prière.
Je crains pour vous, pour moi. Jeune immortel,
Restez encor: votre seule présence
Repoussera l'ennemi qui s'avance.

SATAN.

Mes fonctions me rappellent au ciel.

ADAM.

Goûtez du moins ces fruits que sans culture
Offre à nos mains la prodigue nature.

---

[38] The line echoes the revolutionary call, 'Plutôt la mort que l'esclavage', included in the famous marching song *Veillons au salut de l'Empire* (1791).

SATAN.

Non, pour un ange, ils seraient sans saveur.
Il n'en est qu'un dont j'aime la douceur.

ÈVE.

Et c'est celui qu'on nous défend, je gage.

SATAN.

Oui, sa vertu conserve la beauté,
Du Créateur elle achève l'ouvrage,
Donne à l'esprit plus de sagacité,
De l'ignorance éclaircit le nuage,
Et dans nos sens fixe la volupté.

ÈVE.

Hélas!

ADAM.

Cachez vos regrets et vos larmes.

ÈVE.

Veut-on aussi nous défendre les pleurs?

SATAN.

On aurait dû tout permettre à vos charmes;
Mais d'un bon maître adorez les rigueurs.

ÈVE.

Vous nous quittez, ô le plus beau des anges!

ADAM.

Portez à Dieu nos vœux ... et nos louanges. »

      Pour échapper aux pièges du démon,
Le sage Adam se met en oraison.
Moins effrayée, Ève était moins pieuse.
Elle s'éloigne indolente et rêveuse,
Marche sans but, et ne remarque pas
L'éclat des fleurs qui s'ouvrent sous ses pas.
Un papillon trouble sa rêverie.
Léger, brillant, il amuse ses yeux.
Elle suit donc dans la vaste prairie
L'insecte ailé qui, variant ses jeux,
Fuyait toujours et revenait sans cesse.
C'est vainement qu'elle croit le saisir:
De fleur en fleur passant avec vitesse,
D'Ève il trompait l'impatient désir,
Elle abandonne une poursuite vaine,
Et sur ses pas revient avec lenteur.
Un jeune cerf éclatant de blancheur,
Sort tout à coup de la forêt prochaine.
Son bois est d'or, et d'or son pied léger,
Il ralentit sa course; Ève l'appelle;
Soumis il vient, se courbe devant elle,
Et l'imprudente, ignorant le danger,
À ce coursier sans crainte se confie.
Sur le front d'or sa blanche main s'appuie.
Du cerf heureux elle excite les pas:
Dans les détours de la forêt obscure
Il court, il vole, et sa facile allure
Ne froisse point les charmes délicats,
Les charmes nus qui doucement le pressent,
Et que parfois ses mouvements caressent.
Ève l'arrête enfin; elle descend,
Regarde, et voit l'arbre heureux et funeste.
Elle rougit, répète en gémissant,
«Éloignons-nous »; et pourtant elle reste.
Un beau serpent sur un rameau placé,
Dressant sa tête et son corps nuancé,
Lui dit: « Salut, aimable souveraine.

- Quoi! vous parlez? ô merveille soudaine!
- C'est ce doux fruit qui m'a donné la voix.
- Fuyons, fuyons; je le veux, je le dois. »
Elle fuit donc, en retournant la tête,
Puis ralentit sa marche, puis s'arrête,
Revient, soupire, et s'assied sur les fleurs.
Un bel oiseau dont le brillant plumage
De l'arc-en-ciel réunit les couleurs,
En se perchant sur le plus haut feuillage,
Chante ces mots: « Reine de ce séjour,
Écoutez-moi; je suis l'oiseau d'amour.
Vous êtes belle et vous versez des larmes?
Belle, et vos jours s'usent dans la langueur?
Goûtez ce fruit, et connaissez vos charmes;
Goûtez l'amour, la vie, et le bonheur.
– On nous défend d'y toucher. – Vain scrupule!
Que l'ignorance est timide et crédule!
– Dieu sait punir. – Ce Dieu m'a-t-il puni?
– Non, et pourtant je crains. – J'ai craint aussi.
Ce fruit pourrait, en épurant votre être,
Vous rapprocher de la Divinité,
Briser vos fers; et, malgré sa bonté,
Voilà toujours ce que prévient un maître. »
Il dit, descend, et son bec azuré
À l'imprudente offre le fruit doré
Dont le parfum cause une douce ivresse.
Elle prévoit et combat sa faiblesse,
Deux fois avance et retire sa main,
L'avance encore, tremble, et reçoit enfin…
Dieu protecteur, secourez sa jeunesse.
Vaine prière! Ève, n'achève pas,
Arrête, écoute. – … Il n'est plus temps, hélas!
Toi, qui du monde es la douce merveille,
Toi, qui nous perds et nous perdras toujours,
Mélange heureux de grâces et d'amours,
Je vois l'enfer sur ta bouche vermeille;
Et tu souris, comme on sourit aux cieux!
Et du bonheur l'aurore est dans tes yeux!
Que maudits soient l'arbre de la science,
D'un maître dur la bizarre défense,

Le fruit fatal qui peupla l'univers,
Et la Genèse, et Milton, et mes vers!

FIN DU DEUXIÈME CHANT

===================================

CHANT TROISIÈME.

Un sort malin à la beauté nouvelle
Donne souvent un démon qui l'instruit,
Et qui bientôt lui présente ce fruit
Pour lui si doux, si dangereux pour elle.
Toi, dont le nom est encor dans mon cœur,
Premier objet dont j'ai tenté les charmes,
Pardonne-moi mon crime et mon bonheur.[39]
Combien hélas! ils m'ont coûté de larmes.
Ce n'étaient point les pleurs du repentir:
De mes péchés j'aimais le souvenir.
Mais nos adieux et ma vaine constance
De ces péchés furent la pénitence.
Jeunes lecteurs, peut-être de Satan
Vous enviez et recherchez la gloire.
Ah, malheureux! redoutez sa victoire,
Et préférez la sagesse d'Adam.
  Cet honnête homme achève sa prière;
Ève paraît, et sa marche légère,
Son front riant étonnent son époux.
« Femme, dit-il, d'un ton tranquille et doux,
Dans tes yeux bleus quel feu naissant pétille!
Au firmament ainsi l'étoile brille.

---

[39] Parny is referring here to Éléonore, the young woman he celebrated in his *Poésies érotiques* (1st edition 1778). In thus introducing a personal reminiscence, he is following the example of Milton (e.g. the reflections on his blindness in *PL* iii. 22–55) which had been criticized by Voltaire.

Qui t'a donné cet heureux enjoûment?[40]
Plus agité, ton jeune sein rappelle
Des flots du lac le léger mouvement.
Que le souris sur ta bouche est charmant!
Telle s'entrouvre une rose nouvelle.
Femme, jamais tu ne fus aussi belle.[41] »
Ève répond par un vague discours,
N'ose avouer ses désirs, sa science,
Met dans ses yeux sa douce impatience,
Par des soupirs appelle les amours,
S'offre au baiser, et sa main caressante
Presse d'Adam la main indifférente.
La nuit enfin les invite au repos.
Nus, et couchés sur la même fougère,
Ils se touchaient: pauvre Adam! les pavots
Ferment déjà sa tranquille paupière.
Ève plus tard s'endort; du bois épais,
L'oiseau d'amour descend alors près d'elle:
Il la contemple, et du bout de son aile
Il rafraîchit et touche ses attraits.
Elle sourit; un songe heureux l'agite,
Et dans ses sens éveille le désir;
Ses bras trompés s'ouvrent, son sein palpite,
Elle soupire, et rêve le plaisir.

    D'un pas égal, et lent, et taciturne,
Arrive enfin le trône Ituriel,[42]
Qui, détaché du camp de Raphaël,
Fait du jardin la visite nocturne.
Cet officier des saintes légions
Commande alors vingt dominations.

---

[40] The spelling is maintained to respect the metre.

[41] *Les Galanteries de la Bible* indicate, after Eve has tasted the forbidden fruit : 'Le péché l'avait embellie.'

[42] The angel Ithuriel appears in *PL* iv. The name also occurs in one of Voltaire's philosophical tales, *Le Monde comme il va, vision de Babouc*. 'Trône', like 'domination', is a rank in the angelic hierarchy: cf. 'Thrones, dominations, princedoms, virtues, powers' (*PL* v. 840), following Colossians 1:16: 'For by him were all things created, that are in heaven, and that are in earth, visible and invisible, whether they be thrones, or dominations, or principalities, or powers'. Parny makes much use of the different angelic orders in Cantos II and X of *La Guerre des Dieux*.

Dans le bocage où dormait la jeune Ève
Sans bruit il entre, et du bout de son glaive,
Pour le chasser, il touche cet oiseau
Trop caressant. Sur la poudre en monceau
Si vous jetez une mèche allumée,
Elle s'enflamme; une épaisse fumée
Obscurcit l'air, et monte jusqu'aux cieux:
Lorsqu'au théâtre une trappe à nos yeux
S'ouvre et vomit quelque ombre menaçante,
Le faible enfant, que saisit l'épouvante,
Tremble et pâlit sur sa mère penché:
Satan ainsi, légèrement touché,
Reprend soudain sa forme colossale,
Son front affreux, son glaive, et dit: « C'est moi;
Que voulez-vous? » La surprise et l'effroi
Font reculer la patrouille rivale.
Ituriel veut cacher sa frayeur,
Et d'une voix qu'il croyait ferme et forte:
« Je ne veux rien; mais pourquoi de la sorte
Vous travestir? Pouvez-vous du Seigneur
Braver encor la colère et la foudre?
Tremblez, son bras va vous réduire en poudre. »
On lui répond d'un ton plus assuré:
« Lâche, trembler n'appartient qu'à l'esclave.
Quant à ton maître, il est vrai, je le brave;
Va le lui dire; ici je l'attendrai. »
Ainsi parlant, Satan menace et presse
Les bienheureux qui reculent sans cesse.
Toujours railleur, indévot, et hautain,
Il les repousse aux portes du jardin.
Fort à propos quelques anges arrivent;
Deux bataillons s'ébranlent et les suivent;
Et Raphaël, à leur tête placé,
Dit à Satan: « Quel projet insensé,
Fier ennemi, dans les cieux te ramène?
– Mons.[43] Raphaël, pour tes lâches soldats
Garde cet air et cette voix hautaine.

---

[43] *Mons.* is an abbreviation of *Monsieur* used in common parlance as a sign of disrespect.

Tu me connais[44] ainsi parle plus bas.
De mes desseins je ne rends jamais compte.
– Mais sans congé pourquoi briser tes fers?
Pourquoi sortir du gouffre des enfers
Où tu cachais ta défaite et ta honte?
– Point de réponse à sottes questions.
Et toi, bavard, avec ces légions
Pourquoi quitter le ciel qui te réclame?
– Pour obéir aux ordres de mon roi.
– Des purs esprits noble et brillant emploi;
Garder un homme, et veiller sur sa femme!
– Ange intraitable et rebelle obstiné,
À quels dangers ton audace te livre!
Fuis, ou bientôt par mes troupes cerné…
– Seul à l'écart oseras-tu me suivre?
– Un général ne peut combattre ainsi.
– Eh bien, mon cher, nous nous battrons ici. »
Terrible alors, altéré de vengeance,
Il veut d'un coup pourfendre Raphaël,
À l'instant même il voit Ituriel,
Qui bravement par derrière s'avance.
Sans retourner la tête, d'un revers
Il tranche en deux ce trône épais et large
Dont le cri sourd ébranle au loin les airs.[45]
Puis sur l'archange il retombe, et décharge
Un coup affreux, qui du crâne au menton
Ouvre sa tête et brise sa raison;
Car la raison, fille de la pensée,
Dans la cervelle est toujours enchâssée.
La troupe entière aussitôt fond sur lui.
Mais il évite un combat inutile.
D'un air vainqueur, d'un pas lent et tranquille,
Sage il recule, et se dit: « Aujourd'hui
J'ambitionne une plus douce gloire;
Je veux sur l'homme achever ma victoire.
Il tient en l'air son glaive redouté,

---

[44] *Connaître* has the meaning of *reconnaître*, to recognize, in this context.
[45] In canto X of *La Guerre des Dieux*, Michael is sliced in two by Odin, but the halves reassemble, though the archangel is not much use thereafter. Cf. *PL* vi. 325–53, where Satan is cut in two by Michael but the wound swiftly heals.

Et fièrement aux anges il fait face.
Quelquefois même il s'arrête, il menace,
Et l'ennemi recule épouvanté.
Du ciel enfin repassant la limite,
Dans ses états il rentre satisfait.
Quel changement! Ô merveille subite!
Des sept péchés trop funeste bienfait!
Plus de désert dont l'âpreté repousse;
Mais un chemin spacieux, qui descend
Entre les fleurs, et sa pente est si douce,
Que dans l'enfer on arrive en dansant.
Satan y vole, et pour lui quel spectacle!
De cet enfer un facile miracle
Changea la face; il admire et sourit.
Un autre azur en voûte s'arrondit.
Au centre il voit l'immense réverbère
Qui jette au loin des torrents de lumière.
Dans ce séjour, les chimistes féconds
De la nature ont versé tous les dons.
Par elle instruits, sur la rase campagne
Ils ont assis cette haute montagne:
Ses quatre flancs offrent quatre saisons.
Sur le sommet que l'aquilon assiège,
Et qui souvent est blanchi par la neige,
L'œil aime à voir ce volcan éternel
Qui fume et tonne, et lance vers le ciel
De longs éclairs, de volantes fusées,
D'autres soleils, des gerbes embrasées,
Et le fracas des bruyants serpenteaux.
Pour varier la scène, des troupeaux
Au bas du mont s'égarent et bondissent.
Plus bas encor quatre fleuves jaillissent,
Qui sur les fleurs promènent lentement
Une eau limpide et son heureux murmure,
D'un lait sucré la mousse fraîche et pure,
Un vin exquis et le moka fumant.[46]
À l'appétit s'offrent incessamment

---

[46] Cf. the four rivers of Paradise (Genesis 2:10–14) and the 'four infernal rivers' (*PL* ii. 375) which Milton borrowed from the four rivers of the underworld in Virgil's *Æneid*, Book VI.

L'ortolan gras, les truffes, les suprêmes,
De Périgueux les succulents pâtés.
Et ceux encor dans Strasbourg imités,
Les turbotins, les fondus et les crèmes,
Sorbets et punch, glaces et marasquin,
Tout ce qui plaît, tout ce qui damne enfin.
Là triomphaient la Luxure et ses filles.
Sur le gazon ces danseuses gentilles
Forment des pas: leurs souples mouvements,
Leur nudité, leurs formes arrondies,
Ces sauts légers, ces culbutes hardies,
Des spectateurs font toujours des amants.
D'autres plus loin attendent sous l'ombrage:
Leur bouche humide avertit le désir,
Leur voix caresse, et leur libre langage
Offre aux passants l'ivresse du plaisir.
D'autres nageaient; mais légères et nues,
Sur le cristal avec grâce étendues,
Facilement elles fendent les eaux.
Voyez flotter ces deux globes rivaux…
Il n'est plus temps; tout à coup renversées,
D'un sein qui s'enfle elles montrent les lis,
Et doucement par l'onde balancées,[47]
Livrent à l'œil des appas plus chéris.
Mais il en est qu'amour rendra sensibles.
Leur front alors connaîtra la pudeur:
Elles iront au fond des bois paisibles
Cacher leur trouble et leur premier bonheur.
    Satan paraît; la trompette éclatante,
L'aigre clairon et le bruyant tambour
Au vaste enfer annoncent son retour.
Plus de baisers; sous l'enseigne flottante
Chefs et soldats sont aussitôt rangés.
Il conte alors son pénible voyage,
Le bel Éden, ses succès, son courage;
Puis il ajoute: « Amis, déjà vengés,
Nous le serons encor mieux, je l'espère.
Mais votre bras me devient nécessaire:

---

[47] We have corrected a typo and inserted an s here.

Il faut du ciel occuper les guerriers.
Suivez-moi donc; partageons les lauriers. »
　　Les inviter à reprendre les armes,
C'est au gourmand offrir un bon repas,
Au vieux pécheur de novices appas,
Et des catins à de robustes Carmes.[48]
Voyez leur joie et leur avidité.
Ils sont partis; comme eux part la Luxure,
Se promettant quelque heureuse aventure:
Dans les enfers on la nomme Astarté.
Partant aussi, ses filles libertines,
Au lieu de glaives, ont des rameaux fleuris,
Et sous les fleurs se cachent des épines.
Parfois dit-on, une épine a son prix.
　　C'était l'instant qui précède l'aurore.
Le camp nombreux qu'a laissé Raphaël
Obéissait à l'archange Itoël.
Sur les guerriers l'ombre planait encore,
Et prolongeait leur tranquille sommeil
Quel bruit soudain et quel fâcheux réveil!
Dans la nuit brille, ainsi qu'une comète,
Du fier Satan la lumineuse aigrette.
De tous côtés la peur, des cris confus;
De tous côtés les anges éperdus,
Des généraux la voix retentissante,
Des officiers la bravoure impuissante,
Les coups pleuvants, les Trônes pourfendus,
Les Séraphins sur l'arène étendus,
L'horreur enfin, l'épouvante, la fuite,
Et du vainqueur la sanglante poursuite.
« Brave Moloch, dit Satan, c'est assez;
De nos guerriers modère la vaillance;
Prends poste ici. Les ennemis chassés
Laissent Éden sans garde et sans défense;
J'y vole seul: et toi, ferme en ce lieu,
N'attaque point; je reviendrai dans peu. »
Il part, d'Adam méditant la défaite.
Le dur Moloch, affamé de combats,

---

[48] Carmelite monks had a reputation for lust.

Pourtant s'arrête, ordonne la retraite,
Et dans le camp renferme ses soldats.
    Au haut des cieux on voit alors paraître
Des bataillons qu'au secours d'Itoël
Conduit trop tard le brave Gabriel.
« Qui d'entre vous ira les reconnaître?
A dit Moloch. – Moi, répond Astarté. »
Et sur-le-champ, de ses filles suivie,
Armant sa main d'une branche fleurie,
Elle s'avance avec légèreté.
En souriant, la brigade ennemie,
De ces démons contemple la beauté,
Les doux regards et l'air de volupté.
Viens, Gabriel, Astarté te défie.
Lœta, Smiline, Osculette et Kissmie,[49]
Toutes enfin, avec de longs rameaux,
Frappent gaîment soldats et généraux.
Anges, fuyez! Mais leur désir dévore
La nudité de ces contours charmants,
Nouveaux pour eux, et qu'à leurs yeux encore
Développaient de libres mouvements.
Frappés d'abord, attaqués par ces belles,
Nos imprudents attaquent à leur tour.
Sans les frapper, ils avancent sur elles.
Dans leurs regards brille un coupable amour;
Des feux impurs dans leurs veines circulent.
Pour achever ce glorieux succès,
Adroitement les friponnes reculent,
Et bien ou mal défendent leurs attraits.
On les poursuit, on les serre de près.
Frappant toujours, et toujours caressées,
À droite, à gauche, elles vont dispersées,
Puis dans la Lune, et Mercure et Vénus,
En renégats changent tous les élus.[50]
    Gabriel seul combat avec sagesse.
Sa main repousse Astarté qui le presse.

---

[49] The invented names can be likened to *Happy* (Laeta) and *Little kiss* (Oscula + ette, the French diminutive), in Latin, and to *Smiling* and *Kiss me* in English.
[50] The fight recalls scenes of *La Guerre des Dieux* in which Biblical characters come face to face with mythological creatures.

Il se permet quelques propos galants;
Mais devant elle il recule à pas lents.
Les deux rivaux traversent un nuage
Que dans ce lieu pousse un heureux hasard.
Un seul instant suffit pour ce passage:
Que font-ils donc, et pourquoi ce retard?
N'attendez pas que ma muse raconte
Ce qu'elle ignore. Après un doux traité,
Le bel Archange au paradis remonte,
Et vers les siens redescend Astarté.

FIN DU TROISIÈME CHANT

================================

CHANT QUATRIÈME.

———

Te voilà donc, pure et brillante aurore?
Va, je maudis la rose[51] de tes doigts
Que les rimeurs fanèrent tant de fois;
Je hais les vers que tes pleurs font éclore.
Du bel Éden pourquoi réveilles-tu
Les possesseurs? Ils dormiraient encore,
Toujours peut-être, et n'eussent rien perdu.
Femme qui dort conserve sa vertu.
　« Mon cher Adam, vois ces deux tourterelles.
Dans leurs baisers quelle vivacité,
Quelle tendresse et quelle volupté!
C'est le plaisir qui fait frémir leurs ailes. »
Adam regarde et dit avec candeur;
« Je crois plutôt, Ève, qu'à leur manière
Ces oiseaux-là bénissent le Seigneur.

---

[51] There is a play on words, Parny referring to *la rose* (the rose as a flower) which withers, rather than *le rose* (the colour pink) of Dawn's fingers in the Homeric tradition.

– Vois du taureau la fougue et la vigueur:
À la génisse il vole… – Autre prière.
– Prions comme eux. – Pour le louer, ma chère,
Dieu nous donna la parole et le chant.
Offrons-lui donc l'hymne reconnaissant
Qu'il nous apprit dans la leçon dernière. »
Ève, à ce mot, s'éloigne avec dépit,
Marche au hasard, et rêveuse elle dit:
« Si mon époux garde son ignorance,
Que faire, hélas! de ma vaine science? »
Dans ses beaux yeux roulent des pleurs naissants;
Un désir vague agite tous ses sens.
L'éclat du jour, cet azur sans nuage,
Ce frais vallon, ces suaves odeurs,
Rien ne lui plaît. Loin des bosquets de fleurs
Elle aperçoit un lieu triste et sauvage,
Des rochers nus, des arbres sans feuillage.
Ève, craignez ce piège du démon.
Elle s'assied l'imprudente, et sous elle
Satan fait naître une plante nouvelle
Dont la vertu fécondera Junon.[52]
Présent fatal! Cette fleur étrangère
Des voluptés touche le sanctuaire,
Et par degrés éveille une autre fleur,[53]
Ève bientôt devine le bonheur,
L'oiseau d'amour paraît; il lui présente
Le fruit mortel qu'elle a trouvé si doux.
Elle sourit, et sa main caressante
Flatte l'oiseau placé sur ses genoux.
Il les couvrait d'une aile frémissante.
Il ose plus; de son bec amoureux,
L'azur effleure un sein voluptueux;
Et de la bouche il entrouvre la rose.[54]
Ève soupire, et dans son trouble heureux

---

[52] In Ovid's *Metamorphoses*, Flora tells how Juno, jealous of Jupiter having given birth to Minerva without her involvement, also wished to have a child on her own; a flower made her bear the god Mars.

[53] One of the traditional names for the clitoris, in French, is *la rose* (the rose).

[54] In canto II of *La Guerre des Dieux*, we are shown a similar scene in which the Holy Spirit, in the shape of a dove, apparently seduces the Virgin Mary.

Sur une main sa tête se repose.
Ainsi Léda se penche mollement,
Lorsque d'un cygne elle fait un amant.
Mais du plaisir, avant cette aventure,
Léda connut le trait doux et fatal:
Ève l'ignore, et toute la nature
Semble répondre à son cri virginal.
L'herbe soudain couvre[55] la roche aride;
L'arbre agité fleurit; une eau limpide
En jets s'élance à travers les rameaux;
Des chants lointains éveillent les échos.
Ève entend peu ce concert d'allégresse:
La volupté pour elle est une ivresse,
Et son repos est encor le bonheur.
Faible et charmante, elle rouvre avec peine
Des yeux chargés d'une humide langueur,
Et ne voit plus... ô surprise! ô douleur!
Qui peut causer cette fuite soudaine?
« Oiseau chéri, disait-elle, reviens;
Et tes plaisirs égaleront les miens. »
Du bon Adam alors la voix résonne.
Ève rougit, elle hésite un moment,
Puis se rassure, et court légèrement
Vers cet époux que son absence étonne.
Elle tenait dans ses mains le doux fruit.
À cet aspect, Adam frissonne et fuit,
S'arrête ensuite, et dit: « Femme coupable,
As-tu goûté ce poison? – J'ai fait mieux,
J'ai dévoré ce fruit délicieux.
– Ô Dieu vengeur! – Ce Dieu si redoutable
Me laisse vivre. – Eh bien, Ève, crois-moi,
N'ajoute point à ta première faute,
Ne touche plus... Tu me glaces d'effroi.
– Que crains-tu donc? – Ô compagne trop chère!
N'achève pas, et d'un maître jaloux
Par tes remords désarme le courroux.
Disant ces mots, à sa femme riante
Il croit donner un baiser amical:

---

[55] *Couvrir* is used to refer to the copulation of animals.

Le Paradis perdu

Dans ce baiser sa bouche imprévoyante
Du fruit proscrit goûte le jus fatal.
Des sucs divins la secrète puissance
Éclaire un peu sa profonde ignorance,
Et de ses sens agite le repos.
Il se refuse à ses pensers nouveaux.
Ève sourit: de sa dent elle touche
Un second fruit; son époux effrayé
Veut l'arrêter, et du poison sa bouche
Dans un baiser enlève la moitié.
Pour lui tout change; il prend un nouvel être;
Il pense enfin, il sent, il vient de naître.
Il voit alors et compte les appas
Qu'il méconnut; des yeux il les dévore.
Brûlant d'amour, mais incertain encore,
À sa compagne en vain il tend les bras.
Pour ajouter au désir qui le presse,
Elle recule, et légère s'enfuit
En l'implorant, son époux la poursuit.
Ève bientôt ralentit sa vitesse,
Et va tomber sous l'arbre défendu.
Au ciel assis, le souverain du monde
Voit leur bonheur; la foudre roule et gronde;
Mais ce fracas est à peine entendu.
Tous deux cachés sous l'ombre hospitalière,
Des voluptés boivent la coupe entière,
Et sans remords leur main cueille ces fruits
Dont la vertu les a si bien instruits.
« N'abusons pas, dit Adam; la prudence
Dans le bonheur est nécessaire encor:
Des voluptés ménageons le trésor.
Des doux baisers l'excès ou l'ignorance,
Voilà le mal; l'usage modéré,
De ce plaisir par l'amour épuré,
Voilà le bien. » Il dit, et recommence.
    Dans cet instant qui perd tous les humains,
Du Dieu jaloux la première personne[56]
Parle en ces mots: « Chez moi! dans mes jardins!

---

[56] *La Guerre des Dieux* mocked the Trinity for being three persons in one.

Je pars, il faut juger ces libertins.
J'aime à juger; pourtant j'ai l'âme bonne.
Passez-moi donc ma robe, Gabriel.
Veillez, mon fils, veillez: je vois Michel
Du noir Moloch repousser les phalanges;
Autour de vous il reste encor des anges;
Ainsi je peux un moment vous laisser.
Pour mon retour qu'on prépare un cantique.
Le Saint-Esprit pourra mettre en musique
Le jugement que je vais prononcer. »
   Satan, joyeux de sa double victoire,
Et dans le ciel cherchant une autre gloire,
Sur son chemin trouve les rénégats:
Il les rassemble et le mène aux combats.
À ses guerriers campés sur la frontière
Un tel renfort devenait nécessaire.
Devant Michel Baal[57] a reculé.
Moloch plus loin, par le nombre accablé,
Ne fuyait pas, mais il résiste à peine.
Du fier Satan la présence soudaine
Rend aux démons un courage infernal.
Leur nouveau choc aux anges est fatal.
D'un coup heureux sur la céleste plaine
Thammuz[58] étend le brave Zéphoël,
Sous Arioch[59] se débat Abdiel[60];
De Belzébut l'acier perce Uriel;[61]
Baal en deux tranche net Ophiel;
L'affreux Moloch assomme Elitoël;[62]
Enfin Satan extermine Azaël.
Michel de loin voit leur chute, et les venge.

---

[57] Baal is a Phoenician God whose cult is repeatedly condemned in the Old Testament.

[58] Thammuz (the spelling varies) is thought to have been a Babylonian deity: see *PL* i. 446.

[59] Arioc appears at *PL* vi. 371, suggested by a king named Arioch in Genesis 14:14.

[60] The name Abdiel appears in I Chronicles 5:15 and is given by Milton to a loyal seraph in *PL* v-vi.

[61] Although not mentioned in the Bible, but only in apocryphal writings, Uriel has long been considered the name of one of the archangels. In *Paradise Lost*, Milton makes him the regent of the sun.

[62] Elitoël seems to be a made-up pseudo-Hebraic name.

Sur Astaroth il tombe furieux.
Celui-ci pare, et riposte: l'archange
Pare à son tour, et droit entre les yeux
Frappe et refrappe Astaroth qui chancelle.
Dagod entre eux se précipite et dit:
« De ce hasard ton orgueil s'applaudit,
Grand général de cour, valet fidèle,
Ne cherche pas un triomphe nouveau;
Va rassurer le pigeon et l'agneau[63];
Crois-moi, retourne à tes bêtes; renonce... »
L'acier vengeur, que dans sa bouche enfonce
Un bras nerveux, de ce diable insolent
Coupe la voix, perce la gorge impure,
Et par la nuque il ressort tout sanglant.
Avec fracas Dagod tombe, exhalant
Un souffle infect et sa dernière injure.
Ce double exploit qu'admirent les élus
A ranimé leur mourante vaillance:
De toutes parts le combat recommence.
À la fureur le fer ne suffit plus.
Elle saisit des armes étrangères,
Et sans efforts lance des rocs pesants,
Des monts entiers, des arbres fleurissants,
Et, qui mieux est, des lacs et des rivières
Déjà peuplés de poissons innocents.
Milton l'a vu, l'a dit; il faut le croire.
Michel encore espère la victoire;
Mais tout à coup se présente Satan,
Tenant en main un cèdre du Liban.
Soudain sur lui l'archange redoutable
Jette une masse au Vésuve semblable:
En se baissant il évite le choc;
Et le rocher, passant loin sur sa tête,
Va renverser Bélial et Chadroch.
Ils sont vengés: Satan, que rien n'arrête,
Perce les rangs, frappe, et ce coup fatal
De la victoire est l'éclatant signal.

---

[63] *Le pigeon* is the dove of the Holy Spirit; *l'agneau* (and elsewhere *le mouton*) is Jesus Christ as Lamb of God. The disrespectful designations also figure in *La Guerre des Dieux*.

Sur les vaincus Chamod se précipite;
Plus de combat; des anges repoussés
Les bataillons sont au loin dispersés.
Voulant encore accélérer leur fuite,
Moloch, aidé de vingt bras vigoureux,
De Jupiter enlève un satellite,
Puis au hasard il le roule sur eux.
Au paradis ils portent les alarmes.
Pâle et tremblant, le Verbe[64] crie: « Aux armes!
Que fait mon père en ce commun danger?
Etait-ce là le moment de juger?
Du saint pigeon les plumes se hérissent:
Sage il s'envole, et dans l'air balancé,
Chantant un psaume où les côteaux bondissent,[65]
Obscurément il prédit le passé.
Déjà croissaient la frayeur et le trouble;
Satan paraît; le tumulte redouble,
Et, les démons sur les pas des fuyards,
Du paradis franchissent les remparts.
Le Verbe alors croit les réduire en poudre;
Mais un mouton sait-il lancer la foudre?
Trop bas il vise, et touche rarement.
Devant l'autel combat la garde bleue,[66]
Satan attaque en vain; en ce moment
Près du soleil passe rapidement
Une comète à lumineuse queue;
De ses deux mains il l'empoigne, et trois fois
La masse lourde échappe de ses doigts;
Mais il l'enlève enfin, tremble sous elle,
Pour s'affermir avance un pied, chancelle,
Et tout son corps lance l'énorme poids.
En même temps sous l'effort il succombe,
Tombe à demi, se relève, retombe.
Du coup affreux l'autel est fracassé;
Le fils du père, un moment renversé,
De ses débris se dégage avec peine;

---

[64] God the Son, in reference to the Word being made Flesh.
[65] A reference to Psalm 68:16.
[66] Between 1793 and 1796, the Vendée wars were fought between the *bleus* or republicans, and the *blancs* or monarchists.

Aux deux rivaux de fidèles soldats
Prêtent l'appui de leurs robustes bras,
Et promptement ils reprennent haleine.
Satan déjà s'écrie: à moi, Moloch!
La garde enfin cède à ce double choc.
Du Verbe dont le courroux se déploie
(La rage en loup peut changer des moutons);
Sans distinguer les anges des démons,
De tous côtés au hasard il foudroie.
Par des farceurs sur la scène amené,
Tel brille et tonne un *peccata risible*,[67]
Qui de pétards est caparaçonné:
Dans ce fracas le baudet impassible
Brait noblement, tient bon sur ses tréteaux,
Dresse l'oreille, et se croit un héros.
En un seul point la comparaison cloche,
Et des savants mérite le reproche:
Les vains pétards que lance l'animal
Aux spectateurs ne causent aucun mal;
Ceux-ci, mieux faits, blessent, brûlent, renversent;
Et de Satan les troupes se dispersent.
    Loin du combat notre Grand-Juge enfin
A des époux prononcé la sentence.
Ils sont chassés de cet heureux jardin,
De ces beaux lieux ornés pour l'innocence.
Bien escortés, ils marchent en silence.
Baissant toujours son front humilié,
Pâle et traînant sa robe de feuillage,[68]
Le pauvre Adam inspire la pitié.
Moins abattue, Ève plaît davantage.
Elle a jeté l'informe vêtement
Qu'elle reçut de la bonté céleste,
Et sa pudeur conserve seulement

---

[67] 'Peccata' is an archaic word meaning both 'sin' and 'donkey': the donkey, which is often beaten, was called 'peccata' in an anticlerical allusion to Christ, 'qui tollis peccata mundi' (who takest away the sins of the world). A 'peccata' could also mean a combat staged between a donkey and some dogs. Here Parny appears to indicate a carnivalesque ceremony in which a donkey ('baudet') – an animal to which Voltaire gave a key role in *La Pucelle* – had fire-crackers attached to its body.

[68] *Les Galanteries de la Bible* refer to Adam and Eve wearing 'robes de feuillage'.

De pampre vert une feuille modeste.
En la voyant, les anges attendris
Disent tout haut et tout bas: Qu'elle est belle!
Ces mots si doux ranimaient ses esprits,
Et consolaient sa disgrâce cruelle.
     Le Juge alors remonte dans les cieux.
Il était temps: les démons furieux
Bravaient le Verbe et sa foudre amortie.
Ammos, en hâte, arrivant des enfers,
Les rassurait contre un nouveau revers.
Son art triomphe, et l'heureuse chimie
Au feu du ciel oppose un feu rival.
Elle a trouvé le salpêtre fatal
Qui lance au loin la mort et le ravage.
Des Séraphins qu'importe le courage?
Du Saint-Esprit qu'importent les versets,
Et de Fanfan[69] la bêlante colère!
Leur voix s'éteint dans le bruit des mousquets,
Et les canons répondent au tonnerre.
Ils allaient fuir; le Père arrive, et dit:
« Cher Saint-Esprit, où donc est votre esprit?
Pour conserver le céleste royaume,
Vous le quittiez? brillant sujet de psaume!
Des goupillons, morbleu, des goupillons;
Et d'eau bénite inondez les démons. »
     On obéit à sa voix magistrale.
De toutes parts sur la troupe infernale
De l'onde sainte on verse des torrents.
Qu'oppose Ammos à ces feux dévorants?
Rien; leur nature échappe à la chimie.
Les noirs démons sous la brûlante pluie
Hurlent d'effroi, de rage, et de douleur.
Le seul Satan résiste au feu vainqueur,
D'un pistolet arme sa main impie,
Et sur l'autel il saute; bon lecteur,
Ne craignez rien; le Papa qu'il ajuste
Heureusement tourne sa tête auguste,

---

[69] As his 'bêlante colère' indicates, *Fanfan* is a disrespectful name for Jesus, possibly a corruption of 'enfant'.

Le plomb sifflant effleure son menton,
Et coupe net sa barbe vénérable[70];
Au même instant, armé du goupillon,
Cent mille bras repoussent le coupable.
« Messieurs, dit-il, de fuir je rougis peu.
J'ai retouché votre œuvre favorite:
Malgré la foudre, et malgré l'eau bénite,
Le premier homme est homme enfin; adieu. »
    Ce premier homme, inquiet et sans guide,
Errait alors au milieu des déserts.
Triste, il s'assied sur une mousse aride,
Et de ses yeux coulent des pleurs amers.
« Quel changement! dit-il; Dieu nous repousse.
Jardin fécond, sans soins entretenu,
Fruits délicats, paresse longue et douce:
Ruisseau de miel, nous avons tout perdu. »
Oui, mais aussi nous gagnons quelque chose,
Dit la jeune Ève, et son souris propose
Le don d'amour. Prompt à se résigner,
Entre ses bras l'heureux Adam la presse,
Brûle, jouit, et, dans sa folle ivresse,
Il répétait: Perdre ainsi, c'est gagner.[71]

FIN DU QUATRIÈME CHANT

---

[70] In canto VI of *La Guerre des Dieux*, God the Father stresses the importance of his beard as a sign of his authority.

[71] A similar sentiment is expressed at the end of *Les Galanteries de la Bible* after the couple has been expelled from Paradise: 'Ève, tu m'aimes, je t'adore, / Et le baiser nous reste encore; / Crois-moi, voilà le paradis.'

Further Reading

We have only included texts mentioned in the introduction, general presentations of Parny and recent articles. For further details, we refer the reader to Catriona Seth, *Les poètes créoles du XVIIIe siècle. Parny – Bertin – Léonard* (Rome and Paris: Memini, 1998).

General Studies on Parny

Barquissau, Raphaël, *Les Poètes créoles du XVIIIe siècle* (Paris: Jean Vigneau, 1949)

Sainte-Beuve, Charles-Augustin, 'Parny', in *Portraits contemporains*, 5 vols (Paris: Calmann Lévy, 1889), iv. 423–70 (first published in the *Revue des Deux Mondes*, 1844)

Seth, Catriona, *Évariste Parny (1753–1814)*, thèse, Université de Paris-Sorbonne (Paris IV), 1995, sous la direction de Sylvain Menant

Studies of Parny's anticlerical texts

Apostolidès, J.-M., 'Quand les dieux font la guerre', *Liberté*, 27 (October 1965), pp. 111–20

Gillet, Jean, 'Un Satan progressiste: le *Paradis perdu* de Parny', *Le Paradis perdu dans la littérature française: De Voltaire à Chateaubriand* (Paris: Klincksieck, 1975), pp. 495–99

Robertson, Ritchie, *Mock-Epic Poetry from Pope to Heine* (Oxford : Oxford University Press, 2009), pp. 283–321

Studies of other texts by Parny

Chansons madécasses

Favre, Yves-Alain, 'Parny et l'art du poème en prose: *Chansons madécasses*', *Cahiers Roucher – André Chénier*, no. 12 (1992), pp. 35–43

Meitinger, Serge, 'Les *Chansons madécasses* d'Évariste Parny. Exotisme et libération de la forme poétique', *Cahiers CLRH – CIRAOI (Centre de Recherches Littéraires et Historiques – Centre Interdisciplinaire de Recherches Afro-Indian-Océaniques)*, 5 (1988), pp. 295–304

Seth, Catriona, 'Les *Chansons madécasses* de Parny: une poésie des origines aux origines du poème en prose', in *Aux origines du poème en prose: la prose poétique*, ed. by Nathalie Vincent-Munnia (Paris: Champion, 2003), pp. 448–57

Poésies érotiques

Guitton, Édouard, 'Deux Laclos en miniature: Bertin, Parny et leurs amours', *Littérature et séduction. Mélanges offerts à Laurent Versini*, ed. by Roger Marchal, François Moureau and Michèle Crogiez (Paris: Klincksieck, 1997), pp. 839–50

Seth, Catriona, 'Le corps d'Eléonore: réflexions sur les *Poésies érotiques* du chevalier de Parny', in *Roman*, no. 25 (1988), pp. 73–78

Seth, Catriona, 'Entre autobiographie et roman en vers: les *Poésies érotiques*', in *Autobiographie et fiction romanesque autour des 'Confessions'*, ed. by Jacques Domenech (Nice: Presses universitaires, 1997), pp. 171–79

Miscellanea

Bensoussan, Albert, 'Voyage du chevalier de Parny', *Études latino-américaines*, 4 (1968), pp. 7–24

Seth, Catriona, 'Un opéra *politiquement correct* sous le Directoire: L'*Alceste* de l'an V (1797)', *Tragédies tardives*, ed. by Pierre Frantz and François Jacob (Paris: Champion, 2002), pp. 169–77

Seth, Catriona, 'L'éloge des infidèles chez Parny', in *Poétesses et égéries poétiques (1750–1820), Cahiers Roucher – André Chénier*, no. 17 (1998), pp. 63–70

Studies of Parny's influence

Barratt, Glynn, 'Eighteenth-century Neoclassical French Influences on E.A. Baratynsky and Pushkin', *Comparative Literature Studies*, 6 (1969), pp. 435–61

Keil, R.-D., 'Parny-Anklänge im *Evgenij Onegin*', *Festschrift für Margarete Woltner zum 70. Geburtstag am 4. Dezember 1967*, ed. by Peter Brang (Heidelberg: Winter, 1967), pp. 121–133

Biographical details

Lemaire, Jacques, 'Parny et la franc-maçonnerie', in *Études sur le dix-huitième siècle*, 2 (1975), pp. 43–57

Parny, Léon de Forges de, 'Évariste de Parny fut-il le père de plusieurs enfants naturels à l'Île Bourbon?' in *Académie de l'Île de la Réunion – Bulletin*, 27 mai 1984, pp. 139–45

Seth, Catriona, 'Parny revisité: les lettres de l'abbé du Chatellier à Rosette Pinczon du Sel', *Cahiers Roucher – André Chénier*, no. 16 (1997), pp. 105–16

Seth, Catriona, 'Chateaubriand et Parny', in *Bulletin de la Société Chateaubriand*, 32 (1989), pp. 80–86

Seth, Catriona, 'Ginguené et Parny', in *Ginguené (1748-1816), idéologue et médiateur*, ed. by Édouard Guitton (Rennes: P.U.R., 1995), pp. 97–103

Seth, Catriona, 'Parny et l'Instruction Publique', *La République directoriale*, ed. by Philippe Bourdin and Bernard Gainot (Clermont-Ferrand: S.E.R., 1997), vol. I, pp. 439–53

Seth, Catriona, 'Le réseau Parny', *Réseaux et sociabilités littéraires en Révolution*, ed. by Philippe Bourdin and Jean-Luc Chappey (Clermont-Ferrand: Presses de l'Université Blaise Pascal, 2007), pp. 127–141

Current editions of Parny's work

La Guerre des Dieux anciens et modernes, ed. by Jacques Lemaire (Paris: Champion, 2002)

Poésies érotiques (Saint-Denis: Grand Océan, 2001)

Chansons madécasses in *Anthologie de la poésie française*, ed. by Martine Bercot, Michel Collot and Catriona Seth, Bibliothèque de la Pléiade (Paris: Gallimard, 2000)

MHRA Critical Texts

This series aims to provide affordable critical editions of lesser-known literary texts that are not in print or are difficult to obtain. The texts will be taken from the following languages: English, French, German, Italian, Portuguese, Russian, and Spanish. Titles will be selected by members of the distinguished Editorial Board and edited by leading academics. The aim is to produce scholarly editions rather than teaching texts, but the potential for crossover to undergraduate reading lists is recognized. The books will appeal both to academic libraries and individual scholars.

Malcolm Cook
Chairman, Editorial Board

Editorial Board

Professor John Batchelor (English)
Professor Malcolm Cook (French) (*Chairman*)
Professor Ritchie Robertson (Germanic)
Professor Derek Flitter (Spanish)
Professor Brian Richardson (Italian)
Dr Stephen Parkinson (Portuguese)
Professor David Gillespie (Slavonic)

Published titles

1. Odilon Redon, *'Écrits'* (edited by Claire Moran, 2005)

2. *Les Paraboles Maistre Alain en Françoys* (edited by Tony Hunt, 2005)

3. *Letzte Chancen: Vier Einakter von Marie von Ebner-Eschenbach* (edited by Susanne Kord, 2005)

4. *Macht des Weibes: Zwei historische Tragödien von Marie von Ebner-Eschenbach* (edited by Susanne Kord, 2005)

5. *A Critical Edition of 'La tribu indienne; ou, Édouard et Stellina' by Lucien Bonaparte* (edited by Cecilia Feilla, 2006)

6. Dante Alighieri, *'Four Political Letters'* (translated and with a commentary by Claire E. Honess, 2007)

7. 'La Disme de Penitanche' by Jehan de Journi (edited by Glynn Hesketh, 2006)

8. 'François II, roi de France' by Charles-Jean-François Hénault (edited by Thomas Wynn, 2006)

9. Istoire de la Chastelaine du Vergier et de Tristan le Chevalier (edited by Jean-François Kosta-Théfaine, 2009)

10. La Peyrouse dans l'Isle de Tahiti, ou le Danger des Présomptions: drame politique (edited by John Dunmore, 2006)

11. Casimir Britannicus. English Translations, Paraphrases, and Emulations of the Poetry of Maciej Kazimierz Sarbiewski (edited by Krzysztof Fordoński and Piotr Urbański, 2008)

12. 'La Devineresse ou les faux enchantements' by Jean Donneau de Visé and Thomas Corneille (edited by Julia Prest, 2007)

13. 'Phosphorus Hollunder' und 'Der Posten der Frau' von Louise von François (edited by Barbara Burns, 2008)

15. Ovide du remede d'amours (edited by Tony Hunt, 2008)

16. Angelo Beolco (il Ruzante), 'La prima oratione' (edited by Linda L. Carroll, 2009)

17. Richard Robinson, 'The Rewarde of Wickednesse' (edited by Allyna E. Ward)

20. Evariste-Désiré de Parny, 'Le Paradis perdu' (edited by Ritchie Robertson and Catriona Seth)

Forthcoming titles

14. Le Gouvernement present, ou éloge de son Eminence, satyre ou la Miliade (edited by Paul Scott)

18. Henry Crabb Robinson, 'Essays on Kant, Schelling, and German Aesthetics' (edited by James Vigus)

19. A Sixteenth-Century Arthurian Romance: 'L'Hystoire de Giglan filz de messire Gauvain qui fut roy de Galles. Et de Geoffroi de Maience son compaignon' (edited by Caroline A. Jewers)

21. Stéphanie de Genlis, 'Histoire de la duchesse de C***' (edited by Mary S. Trouille)

For details of how to order please visit our website at: www.criticaltexts.mhra.org.uk

www.ingramcontent.com/pod-product-compliance
Lightning Source LLC
Chambersburg PA
CBHW070601170426
43201CB00012B/1894